My Beverly Hills Kitchen

My Beverly Hills Kitchen

Classic Southern Cooking
with a French Twist

Alex Hitz

ALFRED A. KNOPF · NEW YORK · 2012

THIS IS A BORZOI BOOK
PUBLISHED BY ALFRED A. KNOPF

Copyright © 2012 by Alex Hitz

Photographs copyright © 2012 by Deborah Whitlaw-Llewellyn
with the exception of those noted on page 353.

All rights reserved. Published in the United States
by Alfred A. Knopf,
a division of Random House, Inc., New York, and in Canada by
Random House of Canada Limited, Toronto.
www.aaknopf.com
Knopf, Borzoi Books, and the colophon are registered trademarks of
Random House, Inc.

Library of Congress Cataloging-in-Publication Data
Hitz, Alex.
My Beverly Hills kitchen : classic Southern cooking with a
French twist / Alex Hitz.—1st ed.
p. cm.
1. Cooking, American—Southern style.   2. Cooking—
California.   I. Title.
TX715.2.S68H58 2011
641.5975—dc23   2012005078

Jacket photograph by Deborah Whitlaw-Llewellyn
Jacket design by Abby Weintraub

Manufactured in China
First Edition

For Pierre Durand,

without whom none of this

may have ever happened

A host is like a general;

calamities often reveal his genius.

HORACE, CA. 65 B.C.

Contents

My food family in Atlanta, photographed in the garden dedicated to my mother, Caroline Sauls Hitz Shaw, Atlanta History Center, July 2011. BACK ROW, LEFT TO RIGHT: *Ronald Ross, Mary-Louise Smith, Jane Mathews, Edwin Orihuela, Merle Smith, me, Kate Sasnett, Larry Couzens, Queenie Stripling Callier, Carolyn McCloud, and Kelly Walling.* FRONT ROW, LEFT TO RIGHT: *Matilda Dobbs, Mary Boyle Hataway, Telena Stripling Saxton, and Peggy Foreman*

Acknowledgments

It would have been impossible to have undertaken a project like this without the love and support of so many different people, from so many varied aspects of my life. I am incredibly fortunate to have had the opportunity to work with Shelley Wanger and Paul Bogaards at Knopf, who were tireless and patient as we shaped this book. The marvelous team at Knopf is unparalleled, especially Peter Andersen, Kevin Bourke, Carol Carson, Sara Eagle, Maggie Hinders, Katherine Hourigan, Juhea Kim, Rita Madrigal, and Ken Schneider, and I thank all of them so very much, as well as my amazing agent, David Kuhn, for helping me make this book a reality. Deborah Whitlaw-Llewelyn is a pleasure to work with and her beautiful photographs speak for themselves. With a heart full of gratitude, I would like to also thank the following people for their fantastic contributions and encouragement:

Bruce Addison, Jen Agloo, Angie Avery, Gayle Atkins, Peter Bacanovic, Lee Bailey, Nora Barcelona, Sonny Barcelona, Lisa Barnet, Sylvina and Bernardo Barosso, Donzie Barosso, Betsy Bloomingdale, Honeybear and Robert Bloomingdale, Chesie Breen, Katherine Bryan, Victoria Brynner, Queenie Stripling Callier, Dara Caponigro, Isabel Cardona, Alonso Carey Sr., Alonso Carey Jr., Jill Cartter, Aimee Chubb, Jessi Cimafonti, Mike Clifford, Larry Couzens, Jennifer Crandall, David Crotty; Alex Darvishi, and the staff of the Houston Country Club; Brooke and Blake Davenport, Barbara Davis, Dorothy Davis, Dimitri of The Tower Bar, Matilda Dobbs, Pierre Durand, Carolyn Engelfield, Ethyl, George Farias, Miguel Flores-Villana, Lisa Fine, Amy Fine Collins, Jim Fitts, Alberto Gonzales, Mindy Grossman, Peggy Foreman, Duvall Fuqua, Michael Foster, Johnny Galliher, Sandy Golinkin, Ellen and Ian Graham, Jim Griffin, Susan Gutfreund, Anne and Bradley Hale, Denise Hale, Elizabeth and Sheffield Hale, Haire, Bobby Harling, Evan Harrel, Ann and Pegram Harrison, Lorna Hart, Nikki Haskell, Mary Boyle Hataway, Brooke Hayward, Steve Heinzer, John T. Hill, Jill and Scott Holstead, Marin Hopper, Gil Jackson, David Jones, Ellen Hale Jones, Judith Jones, Marta Justino, Konstantine Kakanias, Speedy and Kitty Kempner, Nan Kempner, David Kinder, Jeff Klein and John Goldwyn, Billy Kingsland, Keith Langham, Goodloe Lewis, Robert Levy, Marguerite Littman, Ron Litvak, Carol Mack, Jane and George Mathews, Maxwell Maximillian, Zac Mayer, Boaz Mazor, Carolyn McCloud, Patrick McMullan, Heath McRae, Gail Monaghan, Michael Morelli, David Netto, Liz Netto, Marsha Oglesby, Jeff Parker, Peggy Peele, Josephine Crawford Phelps, Jeffrey Podalsky, Suzanne and Fred Rheinstein, Casey Ribicoff, Carolyne Roehm, Ronald Ross, Kate Sasnett, Telena Stripling Saxton, Frances Schultz, Caroline and Robert Shaw, Bobby Short, Eva Sicat, Bill Smith, Dean DuBose Smith, Merle Smith, Mary Louise Smith, Soirée Catering and Events, Wendy Stark, Carly Steel, Richard David Story, Janice and Steve Straske, Gino Sullivan, Annette Tapert, Chari Tennant-O'Neill, Patty and Clay Thomas, The Tower Bar, Mark Tydell, Ed Victor, Connie Wald, Laura Sauls Wallace, Kelly Walling, Abby Weintraub, Ray Welder, Kevin West, Ruth and Hutton Wilkinson, Hiram Williams, Lydia Wills, and Bettina Zilkha.

There is no love sincerer than the love of food!

GEORGE BERNARD SHAW

Introduction

My food story begins in Atlanta, where I was born. As a child in the early 1970s I experienced a genteel world of entertaining, best characterized the way a visiting dignitary described Atlanta at the time: "A cradle of the Old South, a crucible of the New South." In other words, I didn't grow up on collard greens or pigs' feet, but my Southern experience was profound just the same.

Our household was "artistic." My stepfather was a Californian—a world-famous symphonic and choral conductor named Robert Shaw—and my mother, Caroline, a bright, funny, stylish, and capable Atlanta native, was from an accomplished local family. Caroline had been educated in Europe, and although she had grown up in a house where none of the women knew how to cook, or wanted to, she taught herself brilliantly, and, in turn, became an exquisite teacher. "Miss Tastebuds," as I heard her called more than once, "caused" lots of good things to happen in our kitchen. She gave our beloved family cook, Dorothy, the benefit of her exacting knowledge, high standards, and unerring taste. Dorothy's innate ability, combined with my mother's knowledge of European cooking and sheer determination, made the food I grew up with some of the very best in the South.

My parents were proud of their ability to bring diverse groups of people

My mother, Caroline Bryans Sauls, 1964

together, constantly crossing the racial, socioeconomic, and political boundaries of the day. They entertained often; I always knew it was party time when I smelled the Rival AutomatiPerc machine brewing in the laundry room. They preferred lunches to dinners, small to large, and at lunch on any given Saturday in those days one might have found Leonard Bernstein, Aaron Copland, Leontyne Price, or Bobby Short sharing Cheddar Herb Biscuits, Chicken Country Captain, or Shrimp and Grits with the likes of Coretta Scott King, Rosalynn and Jimmy Carter, and Anne Cox Chambers. Their parties were civilized—elegant and pretty but never stuffy: monogrammed linens, family silver, Derby china, French wines, electric conversations, and lots of laughter. They lasted long into the afternoon, and took so much preparation and effort that often outside people

were brought in to help. Then, as now, I never wanted to miss anything, and spent endless hours trying to distract these lovely people from their duties. Luckily, they were all good-natured and wonderful, and, if alive, are my dear friends to this day.

After college I enrolled in what was then the most famous culinary school in the world, Le Cordon Bleu in Paris (long before it advertised on television and had outposts next to the Olive Garden or Applebee's at the Mall of America), and was lucky enough to intern in the kitchens of such culinary luminaries as André

Dorothy Williams Davis, our beloved family cook for forty years, who inspired many of these recipes, c. 1976

Soltner at Lutèce in New York and Michel Guérard at Les Prés d'Eugénie, in Eugénie-les-Bains, France. I then bought a half ownership share in an Atlanta restaurant that is still open, although I don't own it anymore. Mary Boyle Hataway was my partner, and she's an amazing self-taught chef with whom I still spend hours talking about ingredients, depths and subtleties of flavors, cooking temperatures, varieties of vanilla extracts, forgotten main courses, colors of roux, and other general culinary arcana. Many of the recipes in this book are hers, and many we have developed together. She and her staff have generously, indefatigably, advised me on and tested, readvised me on and retested—and

Robert Shaw, my stepfather, a thirty-six-time Grammy Award–winning symphonic and choral conductor

then started all over again—the dishes for this book and for my prepared-food business, The Beverly Hills Kitchen.

As early as I can remember, I was interested in food and entertaining. My

Here I am with Mrs. Bessie Seabrooks Drake, my wet nurse, whose mother, Miss Firefly, left Georgia and went up to Harlem to open an ice cream parlor frequented by Zora Neale Hurston and Duke Ellington.

mother claimed that I planned the menu for my second birthday party: Virginia ham sandwiches on Pepperidge Farm Very Thin White Bread and potato chips. Virginia ham was what is known as Country or Smithfield today, a delicacy available at Atlanta's sole upscale grocery store, Cloudt's. This was 1971.

In those days, in Atlanta, restaurant life was, to say the least, limited. There were "tea rooms" like Mary Mac's or Mammy's Shanty that served passable, plain Southern fare, but gourmet dining didn't quite exist yet. There was

I planned my second birthday party with coordinated bibs, napkins, and tablecloth. The Chagall watercolor in the background was a gift to my mother from Alice B. Toklas.

The Midnight Sun, a Norwegian-inspired special-occasion restaurant downtown, whose interior took vague and watered down cues from The Four Seasons in New York; Herren's, a dark 1930s Jockey Club–like steak and lobster house in the heart of the business district of the city; and the Rue de Paris, the only French restaurant in town. Of course, there were private clubs, which served bland WASPy food, but the best food was served at home. Ours was no exception.

My mother's love of all things French resulted in the purchase, in 1979, of an eighteenth-century manor house in the Dordogne region of France. Our family vacations were spent traveling in Europe, mostly in France, ten francs to the dollar. We spent endless hours driving through the French countryside in search of Michelin-starred restaurants, or a remote château hotel that was recommended

Atlanta restaurant life was, to say the least, limited when I was growing up.

by the *Gault Millau* guide. At every brasserie, bistro, or grand restaurant, each bite was exciting, and excellence was the norm.

Of all the perfect meals, a few stand out. Dinner at Paul Bocuse's restaurant, L'Auberge du Pont du Collonges in Lyon, circa 1982, was, even for a family that considered itself super-sophisticated, a surreal experience—the beauty of the place, the gracious efficiency of the service, the hush of the room, the explosion of flavor in every bite. If Julia's sole Meunière in Normandy was her defining moment, mine was Bocuse's ris de veau, which my mother tricked me into order-

At age three with my mother, who was a great teacher, at home in Atlanta, 1972

ing by claiming that it "tasted like just fried chicken." Sweetbreads have no resemblance whatsoever to fried chicken, but I'm sure I was pulling some sort of adolescent ambivalence; when I tasted them, she had won. They were in a rich cream sauce, its underlying ingredient a classic veal demi-glace with a hint of cassis, and a sautéed fluted wild mushroom on top.

Another of my formative culinary moments came at L'Oustau de Baumanière in Provence. For dessert we were offered tea with mint sorbet, something that sounded as foreign to me as Swahili, and something I wasn't terribly disposed to try. Just bring the *mousse au chocolat,* please! Ever the adventuress, my mother ordered it, and she was generous with bites. By the end of the evening several more orders were delivered for each one of us at the table, the delicious chocolate mousse a distant second to the sorbet showstopper.

There were many other memorable restaurant experiences that I won't mention, but eating in fine and ordinary restaurants in France as an impressionable youth gave me an education that influences me to this day. This period was a golden age and I saw the last of it. Once I could drive, I suggested that not all of my summers be spent in the remoteness of the French countryside, and while my parents would be away for four months a year to escape the

Caroline (front row, seventh from the left), at the Sorbonne, autumn 1956

humidity and the mosquitoes of Atlanta, I insisted on spending more time at home.

After I graduated from boarding school in 1987, a friend of my mother's called to say that she had just been to a nice new restaurant, The Patio by the River. The food was very good, and they were much busier than they had expected. They needed help, and she suggested that I go and see if they could use me. It was a magical spot—on the banks of the only river that runs through Atlanta, the Chattahoochee. The Quonset hut that housed the restaurant had once been an infamous teenage nightspot in the 1940s and 1950s, Robinson's Tropical Gardens, where Buckhead society girls had their first underage taste of liquor and the Georgia Tech boys had been Johnnies-on-the-spot to shepherd them through the process. Before that, it had been

My mother (center), my aunt Laura (left), and Grandmother Betty. Honestly, do these girls look like they'd rather be chopping onions?

Mary Boyle Hataway, who was my partner in The Patio by the River

a speakeasy. Mary Boyle Hataway and her husband, Harry, had opened The Patio by the River and reimagined the space as two distinct rooms: one a country French bistro, the other a red-lacquered, more formal dining room.

To say they were overwhelmed is to say that Waterloo was just another battle. Harry Hataway, an unlikely restaurateur, was a warm but crusty man's man, a former painting contractor who had very different ideas than his wife about running an upscale restaurant. Mary, a highly intelligent sixties *Vogue*-model-turned-businesswoman who had lived in New York and Paris, had taught herself to cook when she worked in the world of finance, where the office politics of the day dictated that she type letters instead of trade stocks. She eventually built a renowned catering business, and subsequently, two beloved, popular restaurants. Now she is a legend—famous for her taste and sensitivity about food and recognized by many great chefs for her contribution to the latter-twentieth-century culinary world. Mary went on to become one of the founders, and then the president of, the American Institute of Wine and Food, the distinguished organization envisioned by Robert Mondavi and Julia Child. She's the person who taught me the most.

I was hired, but because of my lack of experience, I was immediately sent to the dish room to wash the lunch plates. My lone week there was one of the worst of my life—

Mary in her modeling days, New York, 1961

The entrance to The Patio by the River when it opened, June 1987

dingy, odorous, never ending. Harry and Mary had the grace to release me to the front of the house soon after, where I greeted guests for lunch. I worked there for several more summers throughout college, mastering the sauté and grill stations, the pantry, garnish, table service, and the front. My own family was three thousand miles away in France during those summers, and Mary and Harry and their devoted employees became my family. After college, when Harry decided he wanted to sell his portion of The Patio by the River, I was thrilled to have been able to buy it.

In the kitchen, then as now, I felt free. A restaurant kitchen is a great equalizer. The only criterion by which one is judged is what I call the "how fast can he do it well" test. Those line cooks or career waiters couldn't have cared less that I was a partner in the place and cosigned their paychecks. They put me through my paces, and I quickly got one hell of an education in speed, timing, and humility. When a busy kitchen works well together it's the same sensation as speeding along a speed-limitless highway with the top down in a brand-new Lamborghini; when it doesn't, you might as well have taken the bus.

I soon realized I needed more food education. I completed an advanced program at the distinguished Peter Kump's Cooking School in New York, and then set my sights on Le Cordon Bleu, Paris. I enrolled in the Culinary Arts program and soon an elegant and cultivated food language replaced the skills of my on-the-job restaurant patois. In twenty-four weeks I had earned my toque.

The restaurant business as an owner was grueling, and not at all as glamorous as one might believe. All of a sudden, I felt trapped just as Harry had;

everybody stole, everybody drank, and, despite Herculean efforts, nothing ever seemed to change. Mary and I decided to sell the restaurant and it reopened as Canoe, and for years now when the "creek don't rise," it's considered to be one of the best in the South.

At thirty, during my Broadway "career."
Photograph by Ellen Graham

I moved to New York and became a Broadway producer, a movie producer, a clothing designer, and a real estate developer, but nothing quite seemed to fit. I visited many parts of the world, ate in the finest restaurants and some amazing houses, and I took notes. Amazingly, I missed the kitchen. Then, one day, I was able to build a house in paradise, high atop a craggy mountain in Los Angeles, overlooking Beverly Hills, Century City, and the Pacific Ocean. In that house, I designed a gorgeous state-of-the-art kitchen. At last, I was back in the food business, and this time, on my own terms.

I had lost time to make up for, and I began cooking and entertaining constantly. When I first started giving parties at my house in Los Angeles—before it was actually finished, and without hot water or gas burners for at least the first six months—very few people in town knew much about Southern food. They were busy with gluten-free diets, no sauce, and overall ersatz-veganism, complete with bragging rights. Whatever the difficult food fad of the moment is, Angelenos embrace it. I served them the simplest of Southern staples—fried chicken, corn pudding, pulled pork, ham biscuits, pimiento cheese—and now, years later, I'm flattered to find myself at fancy Hollywood parties where fried chicken, cole slaw, corn pudding, and lemon squares are being offered, and feel vindicated. Lesson learned: give the people what they *really* want when you entertain—they can diet the rest of the week.

· · ·

In exploring the recipes for this book, I've gone back to my Southern roots. You will not, however, find moon pies, fried catfish, or pork rinds in these pages. I occasionally had Southern food when I was growing up—it was good, yes, and beloved but perhaps not great—and it certainly wasn't in vogue in the 1970s when America was embracing Northern Italian and Continental cuisines. As soon as I could tell the difference, I preferred bistro and brasserie cooking to Nouvelle Cuisine, which seemed too formal and precious, and always left me hungry.

Years later, after building my house in Los Angeles—and with romantic, nostalgic dreams in my head—I went in search of a Southern heritage and a sensibility that may never have existed in the first place. The old-time Southern cookbooks I consulted featured exotically named dishes based on distinguished culinary concepts: shrimp perloo, Sally Lunn bread, hummingbird cake, Hoppin' John, smothered marsh hen. In my imagination they came alive in a Technicolor Hollywood way: images of cavaliers and cotton fields, Rhett and Scarlett in their Sunday best at the Twelve Oaks barbecue. Unfortunately, the quality and taste of these dishes was far exceeded in their contemplation than in their reality. What happened? Had these recipes just been bastardized by such twentieth-century conveniences as canned soup and cake mix, or were the ideas merely too unsophisticated for today?

I chose to believe the former. When I refer to Southern cooking, I mean Charleston food and New Orleans food—Charleston as far back as the eighteenth century, with marvels like rice, shrimp, fresh fish, peppers, and herbs, and New Orleans from the nineteenth century on, with its holdover French influences, its "cream and butter food," as I call it, and many later Escoffier traditions alive to this day. These two cuisines—the Low Country and the Creole—are the vague antecedents for what my Southern food is now: a new, punched-up version of plantation cuisine.

While doing recipe research I realized that thanks to Julia Child and her ground-breaking 1961 masterpiece *Mastering the Art of French Cooking*, Volume I, America's food sensibility, and certainly mine, had gone down the culinary rabbit hole, never to be satisfied again. The standards that Child introduced in America had changed our collective palates, and those old, classic Southern recipes, part of a history of civilized and elegant living, just didn't hold up anymore. The ideas are great, but the recipes are merely ordinary—markedly bland and just too basic. I think that taste is fugitive, and my journey back through the widely recognized twentieth-century cooking bibles of the South ended in true culinary despair.

I decided to research plantation food from all the Southern states, many of the dishes only still extant in the regional Junior League cookbooks. *Charleston Receipts*, for example, the bible of elegant menus and entertaining first published in 1950 by the Junior League of Charleston, featured wonderful conceits but ingredients and cheats that, with profound apologies to the Old Bay Seasoning Company, just don't cut it now. Even non-gourmets currently can't condone what had passed the tests in 1950: shortening, margarine, seasoning salt, onion powder, MSG, Jiffy Mix, instant grits. Cooking my way through that book, replete with charming illustrations of the town's historic past, was a short-lived endeavor. The same thing happened with other Low-Country and Creole cookbooks. If we consider Alice Waters a visionary for her promotion of local ingredients in the 1970s, it is also true that old Low Country and Creole recipes were way ahead of their time—poetry was made by blanching an ordinary local butter bean, or poaching an indigenous crawfish. However, I could not be inspired by a ketchup-based barbecue sauce or a roux made of Wesson oil. I wanted Southern food, but I wanted it on *my* terms: the strict European standards of quality and technique applied to those grand old plantation traditions.

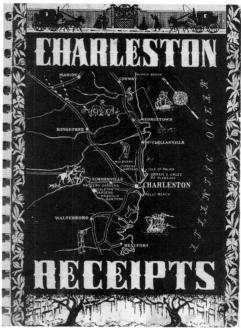

Every Southern cook worth his salt has a copy of this.

That said, I should mention that many of my recipes are not purely Southern—they are resoundingly Southern in their influence, but this collection is a bit of a mix. I've taken ideas from my family, my travels, from excellent restaurants, world-class chefs, from amateur cooks, and those lucky enough to cultivate their food tastes. Where I've reprinted a recipe from another source verbatim, I credit that original source with gratitude, but include the recipe only after it passes the test of *my* persnicketyness. I've developed or analyzed all the recipes using several criteria. First and foremost is taste, which sounds obvious but is more complicated than one might think. I've always tried to make food satisfying on three stages of the palate. The initial taste, or first stage, is the most seductive; if we don't get past that first taste we won't want to proceed. In the initial bite, we identify the characteristic of a single flavor, or the balance of a few flavors, which break down into only four categories—bitter, sour, sweet, and savory. When a taste comprises more than one flavor, the more recognizable each flavor is, the more successful the dish will be as long as they're in harmony.

The second stage is exploratory, and for this stage I try for a depth of flavor that isn't always immediately transparent. The sensation of taste at this stage usually lasts the longest, and the introduction of foreign elements from another taste category is often revealed here. The secondary ingredient can provide a complement to the main flavor that causes the main flavor to soar as a result of the combination. Consider lemon juice: Most people wouldn't like lemon juice on its own, but when added to just about *any* sweet or savory taste it becomes a profound enhancer. Ina Garten would say it's a "magic ingredient." The same holds true of salt as it plays off sugar in desserts, or sour as it plays off either sweet or savory.

The third stage of taste is the finish, or the aftertaste. It should leave you with a happy memory and not a needling reminder. For example, the lemon squares published here (page 307) are an initial explosion of sugar and lemon, but with an undulating element, a supporting player to the majesty of the main character. That support, in this case, is fresh minced ginger, a fragrant, pungent addition to the crust, but not especially recognizable on its own.

Bearing in mind the four taste groups and the three stages of taste, I had my work cut out for me trying to transform the recipes from the "Before Julia" Southern kitchen into recipes flavorful and sophisticated enough for today's palates. I started with a simple but defining element from every proud Southern kitchen: the biscuit. More on that in Chapter 10.

After reinventing the biscuit to my liking, I wanted to reconsider other Southern classics in ways that would please a sophisticated "foodie" palate: fried chicken, corn pudding, Carolina pulled pork, shrimp and grits, Low Country chicken jambalaya, "she" crab soup, fried green tomatoes, cole slaw, peach cobbler, pecan pie, sweet potato pie. My goal was to revive lost dishes, and to update ones that were no longer in favor. I wanted to remake these recipes into timeless classics that even a finicky, mercurial eater with today's tastes might enjoy. As I said before, I entertain often, and I always try to give my guests what I find they really like: comfort food—nothing pretentious, trendy, or precious. Save the test tubes and foam for another time. As I have found with most things in life, simple is always best.

Alex Hitz

My Beverly Hills Kitchen

It's difficult to think anything but pleasant thoughts

while eating a home-grown tomato.

LEWIS GRIZZARD

Kitchen Notes

Notes on Ingredients

1   Never skimp on ingredients: Always buy the best you can afford. The better the ingredients, the better the finished dish will be. I did not say the most expensive; I said the best. Learn to tell the difference. Make sure what you buy is pure and fresh, not processed, made with exacting standards. Please notice that I am not using the word "organic" here although I do believe in the philosophy. Without entering into a lengthy, one-sided conversation about the politics of organic, suffice it to say that I don't believe all of the claims manufacturers and growers make to justify the up-float of the price. In food, you can taste the difference in ingredients, and with the notable exception of tomatoes, and with no disrespect to Mr. Grizzard above, a canned vegetable is not a substitute for a fresh one.

2   Always use salted butter, not margarine. As for butter, sneering purists will have you believe that if you use unsalted butter you might, perhaps, better control the salt in a dish by putting it in yourself. The result inevitably ends up tasteless. I have never yet tasted a dish whose salty taste came from salted butter. I grew up on Land O'Lakes, and it's an excellent product, although

3

there are much fancier ones available now. All the recipes here are designed for salted butter, even though they may not specifically say so, and let's just leave it that way.

3   Bakers make many distinctions about flour. I always use all-purpose flour—with the exception of a few cakes in the dessert chapter that call for cake flour—because it's what I have on hand. I don't really bake that many cakes because I am not very good at it.

4   Don't be afraid of salt. The wisdom changes all the time, but I assure you it's the one ingredient that can transform tasteless dishes into good ones, and good ones into great ones. It's essential in sweets. I still use Morton's because sea salt and coarse salt take twice as much for the same result.

5   When a recipe calls for tomato paste, always use concentrated or double strength. In other words, the tubes, not the cans.

6   My favorite Dijon mustard is Maille. Do yourself a huge favor, and find it!

7   Don't use products as ingredients. The only exceptions I make are tomato paste, Worcestershire sauce (in one recipe), and canned pineapple for the Hummingbird Cake. Otherwise, always start from scratch.

8   Read labels: They are eye-opening. . . . If you don't understand the words on the label, you don't want to eat the food inside.

9   Homemade stocks are always best, but if you don't have time to make them organic bases are perfectly acceptable. Try the Better Than Bouillon brand. Please don't use bouillon cubes as most of them have MSG in them.

10 A note on oil: For vinaigrettes, I almost always use plain, tasteless vegetable oil. There are many varieties, so use the one you feel most comfortable with, but it's worth a mention that whenever I try canola oil for dressings, I always throw the finished product out. For me, it's too strongly flavored. Same thing with olive oil. With the noted exception of 1, 2, 3 Vinaigrette (page 140), I find olive oil way too pungent. The vinaigrettes in France are the same; olive oil is reserved only for times when you really want that strong flavor.

Notes on Cookware and Equipment

1   Buy the best cookware you can afford. Steel and copper are the best heat conductors. I like All-Clad and Le Creuset, which is enamel. Cookware should be seen as an investment as, if it's good, it will last forever, and you will have it for the rest of your life. Every time you cook, you will notice its quality or lack thereof.

2   Throw away thin, cheap baking sheets. They burn things. Buy heavy stainless steel ones from www.chefsresource.com, or your local restaurant supply store.

3   Buy excellent chef knives, like Wüsthof or Henckels, both of which fall into the "they will last forever" category. If you learn to properly use them, they will make your food life much easier. They are available online and in stores everywhere. There is nothing worse than a cheap, bad knife that won't even

cut butter. You must keep them sharp, which the manufacturer can tell you how to do better than I can.

4   Buy a large KitchenAid stand mixer. They are virtually indestructible, do everything, and you will have it always.

5   The food processor is invaluable. Cuisinart makes a very good one. It's your friend, so be sure you know how to use it.

6   Buy a scale, either digital or analog.

7   There's a huge difference between wet and dry measures. Buy measuring cups for both and use them accordingly.

8   You will need a large cast-iron skillet. I find that its heat conduction is head and shoulders above its competitors, and, for making many Southern delicacies, the lifelong seasoning that occurs from use is invaluable. It is also great for frying as it keeps the oil at a constant temperature. Make sure you carefully follow the guidelines for its ongoing care listed on the package—if you don't it will rust and be completely useless as a cooking implement.

9   Only you know how your ovens work: they may be slow or fast. Always check the cooking times and adjust the recipes accordingly.

Notes on Techniques, Philosophies, and General Control-Freak Miscellanea

1   Beware of too much description in a restaurant dish or "daily special" as you go out in the wide world—it's either a way to use up leftovers, or the result of a sophomoric chef. In either case, the hyper-described dish with fourteen flavors is not the one you'll want to order.

2   Having said that, you may find my recipes have many ingredients or steps. Even if a step or ingredient seems superfluous, it's not. I have tested these recipes over and over and if there is a step or an ingredient that you question, just do it my way first, and change the recipe to your liking if you so choose

next time. I can't extend you a guarantee if a recipe isn't followed to the letter. In other words, please sweat the small details.

3   I will never tell you that a good dish is not worth a bit of hassle. Some recipes are downright easy, but others may provide more of a challenge. For those that fall into the latter category, they are worth it. There is nothing in this book a layperson cannot do if he or she reads the recipe carefully.

4   Everybody makes mistakes. It's easy to do. If a recipe does not work, do not hesitate to throw it away and start over. I can't tell you how many times I've had to do this. Yes, it's a waste, but trying to fix it will not work.

5   In cooking, as in life, almost every crossroad requires some kind of a judgment call. Use common sense. If you are genuinely unsure of something, never hesitate to ask someone nearby. Everyone has an opinion on food. An alternative view may help you to uncover an unexpected but correct answer in the end.

6   Many recipes in this book call for cooked or partially cooked ingredients, such as chicken or shrimp. There are so many ways to cook these things, each one a personal preference or favorite. I will only tell you what I do. For chicken, nine times out of ten I sauté it in butter. The same with shrimp. I only partially cook chicken—approximately three minutes per side over a high heat—if it's going into a dish in which it will be cooked again. For shrimp, I melt butter in a skillet and poach it with a small bit of white wine or vermouth, until it just starts to turn pink, if it's going to get reheated. There is nothing worse than overcooked, rubbery shrimp. You can also boil either one in water or stock, or cook chicken in the oven. I approve of all of the above. Here are a couple of simple recipes to make things easier:

Partially Cooked Chicken (to be used in other recipes)

2 tablespoons salted butter
2 pounds chicken, breasts or thighs, skinless
¼ teaspoon salt
⅛ teaspoon ground black pepper

(continued on next page)

(continued from previous page)

In a heavy skillet over a medium heat, melt the butter. Season the chicken on both sides equally with the salt and pepper. When the foaming in the pan has subsided, add the chicken and sear it until it is brown on the outside, but still raw on the inside, approximately 3 minutes per side. Remove it from the pan, and let it rest for at least 10 minutes before either dicing or shredding it. Do not be worried that it is still raw; it will finish cooking in the final recipe.

Note: If the recipe calls for fully cooked chicken, saute it another 3 to 5 minutes per side, until it is fully cooked through but still very moist.

Poached Shrimp *(to be used in other recipes)*

2 tablespoons salted butter
2 pounds medium shrimp, heads removed, peeled,
    and deveined
¼ teaspoon salt
⅛ teaspoon ground black pepper
2 tablespoons vermouth or white wine

In a heavy skillet over a medium heat, melt the butter. Place the shrimp in a medium mixing bowl and add the salt and pepper. Toss the shrimp thoroughly so that they get fully seasoned. When the foaming in the pan has subsided, add the shrimp, and then the vermouth. Let them cook for approximately 3 to 4 minutes, until they are just pink and cooked through, but not at all too firm or rubbery. Drain them in a colander, and reserve the poaching liquid to use in the final recipe or sauce.

7   I am very specific throughout this book about the temperature of butter in the pan before it is used to sauté. Please be careful to get the butter hot enough to cook something properly, but not so hot that it becomes "nutty" in flavor and burns. The rule of thumb that I use is the following phrase: "when the foaming has subsided." By observing your pan, you will know when that

happens. Butter that isn't quite hot enough will be a thorn in your side as you try to achieve the proper sear, perfect crust, or desired brownness.

8   I believe that many recipes, with a few notable exceptions, are almost always better if done the day before and allowed to steep in the glory and fullness of all their ingredients. Please don't cook steaks, chops, or fish the day before, but corn pudding, soups, stews, and cobblers can't help tasting better with some fore-preparation. If you do it this way, when you reheat your dishes, make sure not to overcook them.

9   When you're entertaining, never leave anything until the last minute. Do everything ahead.

10 When you choose to make a recipe, in this or any other book, always read the recipe fully before you begin preparing it. Afterwards, measure out and separate each ingredient. After these two steps, you may then, and only then, begin the active steps. In cooking school, this step is called *"mise-en-place."* If all ingredients are ready and portioned before anything else happens, you won't get caught short of something and require a not-so-quick trip to the store in the midst of a fast (burned) sauté or a soon-to-be-ruined boil!

11 It is better to undercook a dish and then test it along the way as you can always cook it more. You can never cook it less.

12 Measure your ingredients carefully. No use ruining a good dish by carelessness! Please see number 4 if you have any questions on this.

13 Taste everything as you are cooking to make sure you're on the right track.

14 Don't be afraid to delegate to your friends, family, or whomever else you can rustle up. Most people love to participate, and it's truly a drag to chop onions, I don't care what anybody says.

1

Hors d'Oeuvres

My philosophy on hors d'oeuvres is simple: less is more. With apologies, I will continue to say this phrase throughout this book. These days, I find hors d'oeuvres just too complicated. They should set the stage for the main course to come, not try to usurp the role.

When I give dinners, I rarely serve more than one hors d'oeuvre, sometimes two, and *never* more than three. They're always passed, small (generally one bite—which all hors d'oeuvres should be), and fairly simple. Hors d'oeuvres should whet one's appetite for more. They're small microcosms of flavor, a tiny burst of sensuality that is there, and then gone. Maybe you should have another, or maybe you should just wait until dinner.

Dorothy's Cheese "Straws"
Which aren't straws at all, but, actually, wafers

ANYONE WHO has ever lived in the South knows what a cheese straw is: a savory, salty cocktail cookie shaped long-ways like a straw, made of sharp Cheddar cheese, butter, flour, and cayenne pepper, and always on hand for that Southern habit of dropping by. Seemingly every household has its own version, and great pride is taken in the exploitation of its subtleties.

Dorothy Davis, our beloved family cook, rarely used a recipe, but I had the foresight to write this one down. The secret to Dorothy's cheese straws is that they featured dried dill and chopped pecans. These days, perfectly delicious cheese straws are easily purchased, but few are as delectable as Dorothy's.

YIELD: *60 small wafers*

1 pound extra-sharp Cheddar
    cheese, grated
2 sticks (16 tablespoons) salted
    butter, at room temperature
2 cups flour

⅛ teaspoon cayenne pepper
1 teaspoon salt
1 cup chopped pecans
2 teaspoons dried dill

Preheat the oven to 350°F. Line a baking sheet with parchment paper.

Place the cheese and butter in the bowl of a stand mixer fitted with the paddle attachment. On medium speed, cream the butter and cheese together until they are light and fluffy, approximately 3 minutes.

Mix together the flour, cayenne pepper, salt, pecans, and dill in another bowl. With the mixer on low speed, add the dry ingredients slowly. This whole process should take no more than a couple of minutes, and the dough will be coarse and dense.

Remove the bowl from the mixer and place it in the refrigerator for an hour. Take the bowl from the refrigerator and pour the dough onto a floured surface. Cut the dough into 3 equal portions, and roll each portion with your hands to make 3 balls, making the balls into logs about 2 inches thick.

Be sure the dough is condensed so there are no air holes. Roll the logs in wax paper and put them in the freezer for 1 hour. Remove the logs from the freezer and slice them into half-inch slices. Place them on the parchment-lined baking sheet, and bake them for approximately 10 minutes, until they are golden but not yet brown in color. Let them cool at least 15 minutes and either freeze them or serve them.

NOTE These will keep in the freezer for up to six months.

With Dorothy on her last Christmas Eve, Chops restaurant, Atlanta, 2006

My Cheese "Straws" (Parmesan Tuiles)
Note: These aren't straws either . . .

WITH NO disrespect to Dorothy, my "straws" are easier, quicker, and infinitely lighter. Try both and make your own decision: there's no way to go wrong with either one. Please note this recipe calls for shredded Parmesan, not grated. Shredded Parmesan, when it melts, will make a sturdier "straw." I pass these little gems around with Champagne, put them in small silver bowls on the bar, or serve them with any hot or cold soup.

YIELD: *16 medium-size tuiles*

1 cup shredded Parmesan cheese, preferably Parmigiano-Reggiano

Freshly ground black pepper

Preheat the oven to 425°F.

Line a heavy baking sheet with parchment paper.

Place a small (1½-inch; I prefer small, but you decide how large you like them) biscuit cutter on the parchment and drop 1 tablespoon of shredded Parmesan into the circle. Repeat, spacing the piles about 1½ inches apart.

Bake the tuiles for 10 to 12 minutes, until the cheese has melted and the tuiles are beginning to become golden. Remove the baking sheet from the oven and, while the tuiles are still hot, grind some black pepper over the tops. Remove the tuiles from the baking sheet with a spatula and either serve them or store them in an airtight container or freeze them to serve later. They will keep at least a week, but I bet they will disappear the day that you cook them.

Gougères

I PRIDE myself on being a fairly disciplined person but have an embarrassing weakness for these incredible cheese puffs. I simply cannot stop eating them. Gougères are a staple in France, hailing from Burgundy, with a similar omnipresence as the cheese straw in the South. Their flaky lightness, breathless beauty, and craggy complexity suggest that a super-skilled pastry chef has prepared them. Nothing could be farther from the truth. They are essentially fool-proof, and exponentially worth the minimal effort they require. They can be served hot or cold, and are just as good when done ahead and reheated. Once you master this version, get creative, and substitute other cheeses for the Gruyère, or throw in some bacon, or sautéed onions, or any herbs you choose, and we'll see just how disciplined you are!

YIELD: *80–100 puffs, depending on the size*

½ cup whole milk
½ cup water
1 stick (8 tablespoons) salted butter
¾ teaspoon salt
1 cup all-purpose flour
6 large eggs

1½ cups grated Gruyère cheese (or ¾ cup grated Gruyère and ¾ cup crumbled Roquefort), firmly packed
2 tablespoons grated Parmesan cheese, firmly packed
1½ teaspoons Dijon mustard
⅛ teaspoon cayenne pepper

Preheat the oven to 425°F. Line a heavy baking sheet with parchment paper. In a heavy saucepan over medium heat, bring the milk, water, butter, and salt to a rolling boil. Add the flour all at once, and begin stirring quickly. Keep stirring until the dough begins to come together and pull away from the sides of the pan. This whole process should take no more than a minute or a minute and a half. Remove the pan from the heat and let the dough rest for 5 minutes.

Using a rubber spatula, spoon the dough into the bowl of an electric stand mixer fitted with the paddle attachment, and beat it on medium speed, adding the eggs, one at a time. If the dough separates, don't fret! It will come back together. After adding all the eggs, increase the mixer speed to high and beat in the cheeses, mustard, and cayenne pepper for about 3 minutes. The dough should be shiny and sticky—gorgeous!

Using a measuring spoon, scoop the dough in 1-teaspoon increments onto the parchment-lined baking sheet, each mound approximately 2 inches apart.

Turn the oven down to 375°F. Place the baking sheet in the oven and bake the gougères for 10 to 12 minutes. Rotate the pan and bake them for another 4 to 6 minutes, until their tops are golden brown.

Remove them from the oven and let cool on the baking sheet for at least 5 minutes before serving, or let them cool completely and freeze them. They will keep for up to 3 months in the freezer. Reheat them, covered, for 10 to 15 minutes at 350°F and serve them warm.

Mushrooms Stuffed with Blue Cheese

THESE ARE easy, quick, and gorgeous. You can substitute hollowed-out cherry tomatoes for the mushrooms, if you'd like.

YIELD: *12 to 14 bite-size hors d'oeuvres*

12 to 14 whole medium mushrooms, stemmed

4 ounces blue cheese (Roquefort, Gorgonzola, Stilton)

4 ounces cream cheese

1 tablespoon half-and-half

½ teaspoon lemon juice

¼ teaspoon coarsely ground black pepper

12 to 14 roasted whole pecans

Wipe the mushrooms with a cloth dipped in acidulated water (1½ teaspoons lemon juice or white vinegar to 2 cups water) to remove the grit. Do not rinse or wash the mushrooms in water as they will get soggy, bruise, and generally not hold up well when stuffed.

In a small mixing bowl, using an electric hand mixer, Cream the blue and cream cheeses together with the half-and-half and lemon juice.

With a rubber spatula, transfer the cheese stuffing mixture into a pastry bag fitted with a star tip. Pipe the mixture into the mushroom tops, neatly and in a pretty pattern.

Place a whole roasted pecan on top, and serve.

Mushrooms Stuffed with Mushroom Duxelles

THIS WARM hors d'oeuvre is slightly more challenging than the previous cold one, but not enough to dissuade you from trying it. It is also excellent for stuffing chicken breasts, beef tenderloins, or roasted quails. You can also substitute it for the Gruyère in the Gougères (page 16). Don't be afraid to use it in just about anything else that could benefit from a rich, savory stuffing.

YIELD: *24 hors d'oeuvres*

24 medium mushrooms

DUXELLES
6 tablespoons salted butter, divided
½ pound medium mushrooms, minced

2 tablespoons brandy
2 tablespoons heavy cream
1 cup minced green onions (both white and green parts)
¼ teaspoon salt
¼ teaspoon ground black pepper

Preheat the oven to 300°F.

In a large skillet over medium heat, melt 2 tablespoons of the butter. When the foam has subsided, add the minced mushrooms and stir.

The mushrooms will release a fair amount of water as they are cooking. When all the liquid has evaporated and the mushrooms are very soft, add the remaining 4 tablespoons of the butter, the brandy, cream, and onions. Continue cooking over medium-low heat until all the liquid has evaporated and there is barely any liquid in the pan. Set the pan aside and allow the mixture to cool for at least 20 minutes.

Place 1½ teaspoons of the duxelles mixture into each of the mushrooms' crowns, rounding off the tops. Place the mushrooms on a baking sheet and bake for 15 minutes. Remove from the oven, let them cool slightly, and serve.

Fried Green Tomatoes
with Pimiento Cheese

AS YOU know, a green tomato is an unripe tomato, not a special variety of its own. In the summer, they are readily available in grocery stores and farmers' markets in the South, and at Whole Foods or farmers' markets in New York. In some parts of the country, like Los Angeles, they are not as easy to find. I order them from the produce guru at my local grocery store, and it usually takes him a day or two to find them. They are worth it. This unlikely combination is an hors d'oeuvre that will knock guests' socks off. I never had fried green tomatoes growing up, and, in fact, only when the movie with Kathy Bates came out did I start thinking about them. Nothing sounds more Southern, except when you add pimiento cheese.

YIELD: *36 to 44 bite-size hors d'oeuvres*

2 large green tomatoes
3 cups vegetable oil
2 large eggs, beaten
½ cup all-purpose flour

½ teaspoon salt
½ teaspoon ground black pepper
½ cup Italian seasoned bread crumbs
Pimiento Cheese (recipe follows)

Cut the tomatoes into ½-inch slices, and then take a 1-inch biscuit cutter and cut the sliced tomatoes into 1-inch rounds. You will get approximately 3–4 rounds per ½-inch slice. Pat the tomatoes dry with a paper towel.

In a large, deep skillet, heat the oil to 375°F, using a candy thermometer to measure the temperature because a meat thermometer won't get that hot.

In three medium bowls—one for the beaten eggs, one for the flour, salt, and pepper, and one for the bread crumbs—dredge the individual tomato slices first in the eggs, then in the flour, shaking off the excess, and last in the bread crumbs.

Immediately after dredging—they will get too soggy if you wait—fry the tomatoes in batches in the skillet until they are golden brown on both sides, approximately 2 to 3 minutes per side. Remove the first batch of fried tomatoes from the skillet and drain them on paper towels. Repeat this with the second batch. Garnish them with a generous dollop of pimiento cheese and serve them warm.

Pimiento Cheese

This Southern staple, in one form or another, is a very easy spread to make and a true crowd-pleaser. I've served pimiento cheese to many a finicky gourmet who greets it skeptically, tastes it reluctantly, savors its deliciousness in shock, and then asks for the recipe. There are endless variations—pickles, pecans, currants, onions, and so on—but this recipe, with fresh roasted peppers and Worcestershire sauce, is the one I always like the best.

YIELD: *About 1 pound (enough for all of those fried green tomatoes, plus an extra sandwich or two for the cook . . .)*

¾ pound red bell peppers
    (2 to 3 large peppers)
½ pound sharp Cheddar cheese,
    preferably orange in color, grated
    (and weighed *before* grating)

½ cup mayonnaise
⅛ teaspoon cayenne pepper
1⅛ teaspoons salt
½ teaspoon ground black pepper
2 tablespoons Worcestershire sauce

Preheat the oven to 450°F.

Roast the peppers on a baking sheet in the oven for 15 to 20 minutes, until the skins begin to blacken and blister. When the skins are fully blistered, remove the peppers from the oven, let them cool for 2 to 3 minutes, and then cover them with plastic wrap and let them steam for 15 minutes (the steam will loosen their skin). Remove the plastic wrap and peel the skin. Chop the peppers in half, discard the seeds, and dice the remaining pepper strips.

Place the cheese, diced peppers, mayonnaise, cayenne, salt, pepper, and Worcestershire sauce in a large bowl and mix them together. Let the cheese mixture chill in the refrigerator, covered, for several hours, or overnight for the best flavor. Pipe the cheese mixture with a pastry bag over the warm fried green tomatoes and serve. There'll be left over pimiento cheese that you just won't be able to stop eating!

Hot Artichoke Custard
(on Toast Rounds or as a Dip)

BLUSHINGLY, I include this recipe, which I am sure will make food snobs doubt my credibility. I am prepared for that. This recipe is a beloved, guilty pleasure, widely recognized and largely referred to in varied Southern regional patois as "Cup, Cup, Can." No proper Junior Leaguers would ever have been admitted without knowing this recipe.

Even though I have tried to make it a bit more up-market by adding some fresh minced garlic, there is no way to imagine that it would ever be an award-winning innovation of elegance. I might suggest that you make your own mayonnaise for this, but it's so good with plain old Hellmann's (Best Foods, west of the Rockies) that, quite honestly, it's just not worth the trouble. Serve it as a dip, or as an hors d'oeuvre or toast rounds.

YIELD: *About 2¼ cups*

1 cup grated Parmesan cheese, firmly packed

1 cup mayonnaise

2 (14-ounce) cans artichoke bottoms, drained

1 teaspoon minced garlic (approximately 1 small clove)

⅛ teaspoon salt

⅛ teaspoon coarsely ground black pepper

Preheat the oven to 350°F.

In a food processor fitted with a metal blade, pulse the cheese, mayonnaise, artichokes, and garlic until they are coarse—5 or 6 times depending on the length of the pulses. Do not process the mixture until it is smooth as you will lose some of the pleasure of eating the delicious lumps of flavor.

Using a rubber spatula, transfer the mixture into a 4-cup soufflé dish. Place the soufflé dish on the center rack of the oven and bake it for 15 to 20 minutes, until the top is golden brown. Remove the baking dish from the oven and let the custard cool for 10 minutes before serving. Serve it with crudités or crackers.

My Smoked Salmon Tartare
on Cucumber Rounds

THESE ELEGANT hors d'oeuvres are quick to make and always popular. It doesn't hurt that they look wonderful; the green of the cucumber is so pretty with the pink salmon flecked with chopped fresh green dill. This is one of the few recipes for which I insist on Perfect Homemade Mayonnaise, as it makes a huge difference in the subtle combination of flavors and textures.

YIELD: *16 to 20 hors d'oeuvres*

2 fresh, medium-size unpeeled cucumbers

8 ounces best-quality smoked salmon, diced

3 tablespoons mayonnaise (preferably homemade, page 126)

1 tablespoon minced shallots

2 tablespoons chopped roasted pecans

2 tablespoons chopped fresh dill, plus more for garnish

Coarsely ground black pepper

1 teaspoon fresh lemon juice

Use a kitchen fork to score the cucumbers lengthwise (for decoration) all the way around, and then slice them into ½-inch-thick discs.

Using a rubber spatula, combine the salmon, mayonnaise, shallots, pecans, dill, pepper, and lemon juice together in a medium mixing bowl. Mix thoroughly. Using a 1-teaspoon measuring spoon, place a dollop of the salmon mixture on each cucumber round. Garnish it with a small sprig of fresh dill.

New Potatoes with Caviar

THESE SPECIAL bites of potato transform an ordinary Tuesday night dinner into a special occasion, make mere mortals consider you a Culinary God, and make the grateful recipient, like a greedy nymphomaniac, want more, then more, and more! I first remember them in my mother's kitchen in Atlanta circa 1977, when, after returning from a fancy party in New York catered by Glorious Food, she decided to "enlighten" Atlanta on such a delicacy. (Glorious Food was way ahead of the curve, not only in the food it served but also in how it was served.) She marveled at her own sophistication, and, in fact, so did everyone else. I still make them often.

YIELD: *24 bite-size hors d'oeuvres*

Salt for boiling water

12 small new potatoes

½ cup sour cream or crème fraîche

2 tablespoons chopped chives, plus more for garnish

Coarsely ground black pepper

4 ounces black or red caviar, whatever kind your budget or taste allows

---

Over a medium-high heat, bring a large pot of salted water to a boil. Rule of thumb: 1 teaspoon of salt for each quart of water.

Scrub the potatoes with a vegetable brush. Cover the pot and boil them for 15 to 20 minutes, until you are able to easily pierce the potatoes with a fork. Drain them in a colander and let them dry and cool.

When the potatoes have cooled, cut them in half, and, with the small side of a melon baller (or a teaspoon), scoop out some potato. Discard what you have scooped out, unless you want to make a small portion of mashed potatoes.

In a small bowl, mix the sour cream, chives, and pepper together. Fill each potato half with the sour cream mixture and generously top them with caviar. Garnish with additional chopped chives.

Crab Tarts

I AM so tired of crab cakes. They are everywhere. Let's not keep up with the Joneses. Discover a new star! These finger-size morsels are crust-on-the-bottom-only quiches. The symphony of flavors in this recipe—crabmeat, tarragon, Gruyère cheese, and green onions—make them eligible for the main role at lunch or the opening act for dinner. They are also very good-looking, which, of course, never hurts. And they are absolutely brimming with crabmeat, so use the best you can, preferably fresh, hand-picked lump.

YIELD: *24 to 30 hors d'oeuvres*

1 stick (8 tablespoons) salted butter
1½ pounds lump crabmeat, picked through and cleaned
6 tablespoons dry vermouth
4 large eggs
1½ cups heavy cream
1⅛ teaspoons salt

⅜ teaspoon white pepper
3 tablespoons plus 1 teaspoon tomato paste
1½ teaspoons dried tarragon
1½ bunches green onions, chopped
1 cup Gruyère cheese, grated
1 recipe Basic Pâte Brisée (page 268)

Preheat the oven to 350°F.

Melt the butter in a large skillet over medium heat. When the foaming has subsided, add the crabmeat and sauté it for approximately 2 minutes, until it is glistening and fully coated with butter. Pour in the vermouth and sauté for another 2 minutes, until the crabmeat is fully coated with vermouth. Remove the skillet from the stovetop and let the crabmeat cool for 15 minutes. Don't stir it too much: it's easy to turn gorgeous lumps into shreds. Beware!

In a large mixing bowl, whisk together the eggs and cream until they are just combined. Add the salt, pepper, tomato paste, tarragon, and green onions to the eggs and whisk them until they are well incorporated. Add half of the Gruyère cheese to the bowl and stir.

With a rubber spatula, place the crabmeat into the pastry shell. Pour the egg mixture over the crabmeat, making sure the crabmeat is covered by the custard, and top it with the remaining Gruyère cheese.

Bake for 45 to 50 minutes, until the custard has just set and the top is beginning to brown. Remove the tart from the oven and let it cool for at least 30 minutes. After it has cooled, cut it into finger-size squares, for hors d'oeuvres, or into larger pieces if you plan to serve them as a first course or main dish. These tarts can be served warm or cold.

Caramelized Bacon (Millionaire's Bacon)

IT'S AMAZING to me how many New York parties start with bacon. This recipe was made famous by Bill Blass (more about him later) who was well known not only as a celebrated fashion designer, but also as an excellent host who served superb simple food. I only serve this treat occasionally, but guests are genuinely happy when I do.

YIELD: *24 to 32 bite-size hors d'oeuvres*

½ pound thick-cut bacon, at room temperature

1 cup (packed) dark brown sugar

Preheat the oven to 250°F.

Place the brown sugar in a shallow baking dish. Dredge individual bacon slices on both sides in the brown sugar, patting the sugar down if necessary to make it stick.

Place the sugared slices on a heavy baking sheet. Bake them for 40 to 50 minutes, until the bacon is caramelized and crisp. Remove the baking sheet from the oven and let it cool. When the bacon has cooled, break it into bite-size pieces and serve.

Nan's Bacon Sticks

NO ONE was better at entertaining than Nan Kempner. A San Francisco native, Nan came to New York City as a young bride in the mid-1950s, met everybody, and spent the next fifty-odd years, until her death in 2005, becoming an Influential Society Figure, Esteemed Fund-Raiser for multiple causes, Renowned Wit, Thoughtful and Beloved Friend, Style Icon, Indefatigable Hostess, and Talented Party-Goer. Nan gave lunches and dinners that were great fun every week in her glamorous Park Avenue duplex, which had been built for a silent-film star, Carmel Myers, and was rumored to have had a Champagne faucet in the bathtub. Maybe it was an urban myth, and then, again, maybe not. I was lucky enough to go there often. I called Nan's chef, the brilliant and lovely Silvina Barrosso, who, along with her husband, the elegant and warm Bernardo, spent more than fifty years with the Kempners, for this recipe even though I already knew it by heart, just so we could share some Nan stories. She served these and no other hors d'oeuvres, passed around before lunch or dinner. Just like Nan was, they are very chic and razor-thin.

Jet-set icons: Johnny Galliher and Nan Kempner out on the town, Lincoln Center, 1998

YIELD: *12 sticks*

| 12 medium-width bread sticks | 12 slices bacon (not thick cut) |

Preheat the oven to 375°F.

Wrap one slice of bacon neatly in a spiral fashion along each stick, and place them on a grated roasting pan. Make sure the sticks are not touching each other.

Bake the bacon sticks for 25 to 30 minutes, until they are brown and crisp. Remove the pan from the oven and let them cool completely before serving.

Bacon-Wrapped Dates with Parmesan

THESE LITTLE bites are both savory and sweet, and an updated solution to the rumaki (water chestnuts wrapped in bacon, then marinated in soy sauce and brown sugar and broiled) or Devils on Horseback (pitted prunes with chutney wrapped in bacon). For those of you who don't understand that reference let me explain: In the 1930s, '40s, and '50s, there was a "Polynesian" food explosion in this country, propelled by the opening of such chain restaurants as Don the Beachcomber and, more famously, Trader Vic's. These restaurants burned hot for a while, and then burned out. Quite literally "burned out," as virtually every dish was served flamed at the table. Hosts and hostesses across the country had tiki-themed evenings replete with mai tais and rumaki. The secret ingredients in this "Polynesian" food were sugar in one form or another, booze, and pineapple juice. Eventually, these restaurants and their cuisine fell out of fashion. I updated these bites to a more popular current sensibility (Parmesan cheese instead of water chestnuts, chicken livers, and chutney, et cetera). Everyone loves bacon, whether they admit it or not, and I always insist that we have twice as many of these as we need because most people usually end up taking two . . . or more.

A Polynesian temptress, circa 1940

---

1 small wedge of Parmesan cheese,
   whole

12 pitted dried dates
4 slices bacon

Preheat the oven to 450°F.

Cut 12 slivers of Parmesan, each small enough to fit in the cavity of the pitted date. Insert a sliver of Parmesan into each date.

Cut the bacon slices into three equal pieces, lengthwise. Wrap one bacon slice around each stuffed date, then place the dates on a baking sheet. Bake them for 15 minutes. Serve them hot or cold, immediately or later. It really doesn't matter, as they are delicious any way.

Ham and Onion Tarts

THESE ARE actually semi-crustless quiches. The Basic Pâte Brisée crust is only on the bottom of these delectable bites, for stability, when they are passed. I bake them in 13 × 9 × 2-inch pans, then cut them into small square-inch-size bites as an hors d'oeuvre, but the size can be changed for other uses. They freeze beautifully, and I suggest you cut them when they're frozen, or at least really, really cold, because they are much easier to handle, and then reheat them to serve. A bigger slice is a perfect main dish for lunch, or an elegant first course for dinner. I don't like the word *brunch*, but if you like it, serve these then, too!

YIELD: *24 to 30 bite-size hors d'oeuvres or 6 to 8 larger servings*

6 tablespoons salted butter, divided
2 pounds (before chopping) white or yellow onions, medium diced
¾ pound boiled ham, diced
⅓ cup medium dry sherry
4 large eggs
1⅓ cups heavy cream

⅓ teaspoon salt
½ teaspoon ground nutmeg
½ teaspoon ground black pepper
1 cup grated Gruyère cheese, firmly packed
Basic Pâte Brisée (page 268)

Preheat the oven to 350°F.

In a large, oven-proof, ceramic Dutch oven, heat 3 tablespoons of the butter over a high heat. When the foaming has subsided, add the onions and stir them until they are fully covered with butter. Place the lid on the Dutch oven and put it in the oven for 1 hour. The onions will be very soft, sweet, translucent, and limp.

Melt the remaining butter in a large skillet over high heat. When the foaming has subsided, sauté the ham for about a minute, until it is fully covered with the butter. Add the sherry and stir for another 2 to 3 minutes, until the ham starts to curl. Remove the skillet from the heat.

In a large bowl, whisk the eggs, cream, salt, nutmeg, and pepper together until they are just combined. Add the cooked ham and onions to the bowl and stir them until they are well combined. Stir in the cheese.

Pour the mixture into the prebaked pâte brisée and bake it for 45 to 50 minutes, until the tart is set and brown. It can be served hot or cold.

Mini Basil-Parmesan Chicken Salad Sandwiches

THIS IS a flavorful and full-bodied chicken salad that can be served in a variety of ways. Ignore my instructions about making it into sandwiches if you'd like, and serve it on a bed of lettuce for lunch, on a cucumber slice as an hors d'oeuvre at lunch or dinner, or in a bowl as part of a buffet. There's really no way to go wrong.

YIELD: *3½ cups (enough for about a dozen sandwiches to be cut in quarters)*

1 pound boneless skinless chicken breast, cooked medium rare (still moist, but no longer pink) and then cut into large chunks (page 7)

¾ cup finely minced onion, squeezed through cheesecloth

¾ cup finely minced celery, squeezed through cheesecloth

NOTE I hate to be a bother, but the onions and celery must be squeezed through a porous cloth, as too much moisture from either ingredient will make the finished product runny and just plain bad.

¼ cup grated Parmesan cheese, firmly packed

¾ cup Perfect Homemade Mayonnaise (page 126), or store-bought

¼ cup roughly chopped basil, packed

¾ teaspoon salt

1 teaspoon ground black pepper

Chopped parsley for garnish

Place the chicken, onion, celery, cheese, mayonnaise, basil, salt, and pepper in the bowl of a food processor fitted with a metal blade and process it until it's fairly smooth if you are serving the sandwiches as an hors d'oeuvre, or chunky and coarse if you are serving the chicken salad on a bed of lettuce or in a bowl. For miniature sandwiches, I find a smooth consistency best, but not so much so that the chicken salad is unrecognizable as such.

With a 2-ounce ice cream scoop (this is the perfect amount for these miniature sandwiches), put the chicken salad on whatever bread you like, top with another piece of bread, flatten it, remove the crusts, and cut into quarters on the diagonal. Arrange them neatly on a serving platter, garnish with chopped parsley, and serve.

Mary's Chicken Liver Pâté with Michel Guérard's Onion Cassis Confiture

OFTEN KNOWN as Poor Man's Foie Gras, this pâté may be the most elegant combination of sweet and savory I have ever tasted. This recipe is a hand-me-down from Mary Boyle Hataway, and it remains a favorite of mine because it has a savory depth that, when combined with the succulent sweetness of Guérard's onion relish, is unparalleled. It is gorgeous when piped onto small brioche or toast points, and these complex morsels may be just about the most perfect hors d'oeuvres I know of.

YIELD: *28 to 30 hors d'oeuvres*

17 tablespoons salted butter (2 sticks
   plus 1 tablespoon), divided
½ cup finely diced carrots
½ cup finely diced onions
1 pound fresh chicken livers, drained
½ pound bacon

2¼ teaspoons anchovy paste
¼ teaspoon cayenne pepper
3 tablespoons medium dry sherry
Onion Cassis Confiture
   (recipe follows)

In a large skillet over medium heat melt 12 tablespoons of the butter. When the foaming has subsided, add the carrots and onions and sauté for approximately 8 to 10 minutes until they are soft but not brown. Add the chicken livers and continue to sauté until the livers are fully cooked—not at all still pink.

In a second large skillet over medium heat, fry the bacon until it's very crisp. Remove the bacon from the skillet and drain it on paper towels. In a food processor fitted with a metal blade, pulse the bacon into fine bits.

Add the carrots, onions, and chicken livers to the chopped bacon in the food processor and process them until smooth, add the anchovy paste, cayenne, the remaining 5 tablespoons of the butter, and the sherry and process them until they are smooth.

Using a spatula, scoop out the pâté and place it in a bowl, and refrigerate it overnight.

Bring the pâté to room temperature and, with a rubber spatula, scoop it into a pastry bag fitted with a medium-size star attachment. Pipe the pâté onto toast rounds (brioche are the best, I find) and top with the onion cassis confiture.

Onion Cassis Confiture

Adapted from Michel Guérard's Cuisine Minceur

YIELD: *approximately 2½ cups*

2 sticks (16 tablespoons) salted butter

3 pounds yellow onions (before slicing), thinly sliced

2 teaspoons salt

2 cups red wine (any kind)

⅓ cup medium dry sherry

½ cup red wine vinegar

¾ cup grenadine

3 cups sugar

In a large ceramic Dutch oven or a large skillet, melt the butter over medium heat, and add the onions and salt. Cook them for approximately 15 minutes, until the onions are soft and translucent.

Add the wine, sherry, vinegar, grenadine, and sugar and turn the heat down to a simmer. Simmer for approximately 2 to 2½ hours (without stirring) until all the liquids have evaporated. Let the relish sit overnight so the flavors can develop fully, then serve warm or cold.

2

Soups

Winter, spring, summer, or fall, soup is right. I had soup growing up as a first course more often than not in both Atlanta and in France. Ours were always homemade: cream of mushroom, she crab, lobster bisque, and cold cucumber. I am always happy to make soup, order soup, and eat soup. Soup is emotional and physical; it cures things, evokes childhood memories, comforts. Soup tells a story. Hearty winter soup is hearth and home; delicate cold soup in the summer is elegance. It foretells the promise of the main course to come or stands alone as the single event. Few things are as soul-satisfying as soup, and, in turn, few things are as easy to make. There are basic proportions that many hot and cold soups stem from: bases, if you will, and these bases can be tailored for flavorings and components very easily.

OPPOSITE *A trio of cold soups: Red Pepper (page 62), Cucumber (page 59), and Sweet Potato "Vichyssoise" (page 58)*

Basic Hot Soup

THIS IS my basic formula for "cream of" soups. I invite you to experiment with this magic base: adaptable to anything, easy to make, and utterly pleasing. There are four recipes here that stem from this master formula, and once you get the hang of it, I suggest you try your own variations with things like broccoli, asparagus, carrot, chicken (I would normally say tomato, too, except I am giving you the best tomato soup recipe in the world very soon), and whatever else you can conjure!

YIELD: *6 to 8 servings*

4 tablespoons salted butter	3½ cups milk
1 cup diced onion	1¼ teaspoons salt
¼ cup flour	½ teaspoon white pepper
3½ cups very rich chicken stock	1 cup heavy cream

In a medium-sized skillet over a medium heat, melt the butter. When the foaming has subsided, add the onions and stir, cooking them until they become translucent, approximately 8 to 10 minutes. Add the flour and stir the mixture until the flour has cooked through, approximately 1 to 2 minutes. The mixture will be fairly stiff. Turn off the heat.

In a large, heavy pot, over a medium heat, heat the stock and the milk until it is almost scalding. Add the salt and pepper to the butter and onion mixture. Whisk it vigorously to break up any lumps. Bring the mixture to a boil and then turn off the heat. The soup base will have thickened to the appropriate consistency after boiling.

Add whatever cooked shellfish, meats, vegetables, and seasonings (see variations) and stir in the cream. Heat the soup again before serving.

Mushroom Soup

CREAM OF mushroom is Soup 101: easy, delicious, and fast. Use any kind of mushroom you like, but if only regular fresh button mushrooms are available, those are actually the ones I like the best. The more exotic mushrooms—shiitake, morel, trumpet, and porcini—may be too strongly flavored, if one can imagine such a thing from mushrooms. Your guests will marvel at your prowess, sophistication, and ability. Just don't tell them how simple it is.

Follow all the steps for the Basic Hot Soup, and then add the few ingredients below. As with so many other things, including all the soups, in this book, I wholeheartedly recommend that you make them the day before you serve them to let all the flavors fully steep.

YIELD: *8 cups, or 6 to 8 servings*

To one Basic Hot Soup recipe
  (page 44) add:
3 tablespoons salted butter
3 pounds sliced medium mushrooms
5 tablespoons golden sherry, divided

1 teaspoon dried tarragon
¼ teaspoon ground nutmeg
2 tablespoons lemon juice
Fresh chopped tarragon for garnish

In a large heavy skillet, over medium heat, melt the butter. When the foaming has subsided, add the mushrooms and 2 tablespoons of the sherry. When the mushrooms have released their liquid, remove them from the heat. This should take about 5 minutes.

Drain the mushrooms in a colander with a bowl underneath and reserve both the mushrooms and the pan juices. Add all of the pan juices to the basic hot soup base. In a food processor fitted with a metal blade, puree half of the sautéed mushrooms. Reserve the other half, leaving them whole.

Add the pureed mushrooms, the remaining 3 tablespoons sherry, and the dried tarragon, nutmeg, and lemon juice to the soup base.

Bring the mixture to a boil, letting it boil for 5 minutes, stirring constantly, so that it will not spill over the pot or scorch on the bottom.

When it's time to serve the soup, add the rest of the mushrooms in equal portions to the soup serving plates, pour the soup over the mushrooms, and serve. Garnish the soup with fresh chopped tarragon.

"She" Crab Soup

A soup to remember!
The feminine gender
Of crabs is expedient—
The secret ingredient.
The flavor essential
Makes men reverential
Who taste this collation
And cry acclamation!

A Charleston folk poem, reprinted from *Charleston Receipts*,
copyright, The Junior League of Charleston, 1950

CHARLESTON RECEIPTS is considered the gold standard of Junior League Cookbooks in the United States. It's the oldest one still in print. I have discussed it earlier in this book, and highly recommend looking through it for its distinctive Southern voice, as well as the lists of forgotten dishes, compellingly named like the one above.

Until now, perhaps you had never considered whether your crabmeat was from male or female crabs. No, neither had I. This Charleston favorite was further distinguished from "he" crab soup by the addition of crab roe into the base, which is a fair amount of trouble as crab roe is not readily available in today's marketplace. Sticklers always try to have me believe that this soup was made from only female crabs, but I think that idea is definitely an old wives' tale. Here, I have dispensed with this technicality and added apple cider vinegar, vermouth, and Gruyère cheese, and called it "She" Crab anyway. Who's to stop me?!

YIELD: *8 cups, or 6 to 8 servings*

To one Basic Hot Soup recipe (page 44) add:

4 tablespoons salted butter

2 pounds lump crabmeat, picked through and cleaned

6 tablespoons dry vermouth

1 tablespoon apple cider vinegar

1 teaspoon ground mace

2 tablespoons minced lemon zest

½ cup grated Gruyère cheese, firmly packed

¼ teaspoon salt

⅛ teaspoon ground black pepper

Chopped parsley for garnish

In a heavy stockpot, over a medium heat, heat one Basic Hot Soup recipe. In a large, heavy skillet, over medium heat, melt the butter. When the foaming has subsided, add the crabmeat and, immediately, vermouth, and sauté for 1½ to 2 minutes, until the crabmeat is fully bathed in butter and vermouth. Do not overcook, and don't stir too much: it's easy to turn gorgeous jumbo lumps into stringy shreds. Beware!

To the basic hot soup base, add the apple cider vinegar, ground mace, lemon zest, Gruyère, salt, and pepper. Bring the mixture to a boil and whisk thoroughly. Add the crabmeat and all its liquid, garnish the soup with chopped parsley, and serve.

Oyster Stew

ONE OF my great food awakenings was, curiously, not about eating or cooking, but about reading. I am thinking of M. F. K. Fisher (1908–1992), a prolific food writer, self-styled gourmet, and early proponent of foody-ism, long before it was fashionable. Fisher's writings were messianic for me; her essays examine food, its preparation, its ingredients, its seasonings, and its service as one of the "arts of life," and were influential in bringing the joy of cooking and eating into mainstream consciousness. Her first book, *Serve It Forth*, is widely recognized as a masterpiece, but all her writing is humorous, charming, and irresistible. Don't miss her work, and as for this dish, when you start its preparation (and only try this in an *r* month!), I think it may be

(continued on next page)

M. F. K. Fisher, photographed by George Hurrell, California, 1938

(continued from previous page)

just as important to read her seminal exegesis *Consider the Oyster,* about the life and fate of an ordinary oyster, as it is to read this recipe.

YIELD: *8 cups, or 6 to 8 servings*

3 tablespoons salted butter

2 bunches green onions, thinly sliced (both white and green parts)

2 small garlic cloves, minced

2 cups milk

2 cups heavy cream

¼ cup bourbon (use a good one—don't skimp!)

1 cup very rich chicken stock

1¾ teaspoons salt

1 teaspoon ground white pepper

2 pints fresh raw medium oysters, plus 1½ cups of their drained liquor

---

In a medium-sized stockpot over medium heat, melt the butter. When the foaming has subsided, add the onions and garlic and sauté them for 3 to 4 minutes, until they begin to be translucent.

Add the milk, cream, bourbon, chicken stock, salt, white pepper, and oyster liquor. Bring this mixture to a boil for 10 minutes.

Remove the pot from the heat, and add the oysters. They should "steep" in the hot stock for about 3 minutes, until they are heated through fully and are just beginning to curl at the edges. Do not overcook them, and serve the stew immediately.

Lobster Bisque

I ALWAYS call this "Lobster Bisque for Christmas Eve" because that's how I remember it at our house in Atlanta. It's pretty and pink, decadent, rich, and, let's face it, expensive enough to be considered special occasion food. This version underscores luxury even more as it has tons of lobster meat in it. If you can make the Basic Hot Soup (and if you can read, yes, you can make it!), this easy adaptation will be a perfect winter first or main course but probably a bit too rich for the summer.

YIELD: *8 cups, or 6 to 8 servings*

4 tablespoons salted butter
2 pounds lobster meat (claw, tail, body, or fin)
½ teaspoon of salt
¼ teaspoon ground black pepper (to season the lobster meat only)
10 tablespoons cognac, divided

To one Basic Hot Soup recipe (page 44) add:
3 tablespoons lemon juice
2 garlic cloves, minced
7 tablespoons double-strength tomato paste
1 tablespoon dried tarragon
½ teaspoon ground nutmeg

In a large skillet over medium heat, melt the butter. When the foaming has subsided, add the lobster, salt, and pepper. Sauté the lobster meat for about 1 minute, until the meat is fully coated with butter. Add 4 tablespoons of the cognac and continue to cook approximately one minute more, until the cognac is fully incorporated. Remove the lobster from the heat and drain it in a colander over a bowl. Reserve both the lobster and the liquid. And do this quickly. Nobody wants to eat overcooked lobster.

In a medium-sized stockpot over medium heat, heat one Basic Hot Soup recipe and add the remaining 6 tablespoons of cognac, the lemon juice, garlic, tomato paste, tarragon, and nutmeg. Add the reserved pan juices from the cooked lobster and whisk thoroughly. Bring the mixture to a boil and then remove it from the heat.

When you are ready to serve the soup, divide the cooked lobster meat equally in the soup serving plates and pour the hot soup over the lobster.

Shrimp Bisque

THIS IS another easy and elegant adaptation of the Basic Hot Soup recipe. I love to use the concept of "Theme and Variations" with recipes to promote versatility, economies of scale, and general proficiency. You will see this concept exploited time and time again. It works so well: master one, and you've mastered many! As we all know, shrimp is much more affordable than lobster, but in no way do I ever feel that serving this pink treat is a step down. My guess is that you won't either.

YIELD: *8 cups, or 6 to 8 servings*

To one recipe Basic Hot Soup (page 44) add:

2 tablespoons salted butter

2 pounds medium (20 to 30 count) shrimp, divided

7 tablespoons plus one teaspoon golden sherry, divided

2 tablespoons lemon juice

3 garlic cloves, minced

5 tablespoons double-strength tomato paste

2 teaspoons dried dill

4 tablespoons grated Parmesan cheese, firmly packed

In a medium-sized stockpot over a medium heat, heat one Basic Hot Soup recipe. In a heavy skillet over medium heat, melt the butter. When the foaming has subsided, add the shrimp and 2 tablespoons of the sherry. When the shrimp begin to turn pink and are cooked through but still very rare, remove them from the heat. Do not overcook them or they will be rubbery and tasteless. This whole process should take no more than 2 to 3 minutes. In a colander over a bowl, drain the shrimp and reserve both the liquid and the shrimp.

In a food processor fitted with a metal blade, puree half of the cooked shrimp until they are smooth. To the stockpot, add the pureed shrimp, the reserved liquid from the pan, the remaining 5 tablespoons of the sherry, the lemon juice, garlic, tomato paste, dill, and Parmesan cheese. Whisk the soup well to avoid stringiness from the shrimp and scorching on the bottom. Bring the mixture to a boil and turn off the heat.

When it's time to serve, divide the whole shrimp equally among the soup serving plates, pour the hot soup over the shrimp, and serve immediately.

Tomato Soup

THERE ARE so many good tomato soups in the world that I wouldn't include a recipe for one unless it was a true standout. It requires no technique whatsoever, but you should use good-quality canned tomatoes. Fresh ones would take you days for the same result. It does require a small bit of patience, however, as the ingredients must simmer until a full 25 percent reduction takes place to concentrate the flavors, but just go do something else in the meantime.

This recipe is a signature of my partner at The Patio by the River, Mary Boyle Hataway. She developed it in the late 1960s, and it's a classic: full flavored, unique, rich, and delicious. The surprise addition of strong coffee is an inspiration from an old Italian cookbook, cited as the "secret ingredient," that Italians have understood for years.

YIELD: *8 cups, or 6 to 8 servings*

3 (14-ounce) cans diced tomatoes in juice, undrained
1½ large onions, diced
1½ teaspoons minced garlic
1½ bay leaves
1¾ cups beef stock
1¾ cups chicken stock
2 parsley sprigs

¾ teaspoon dried thyme
4½ tablespoons double-strength tomato paste
3 tablespoons very strong brewed coffee
1 cup heavy cream
1⅛ teaspoons lemon juice
¾ teaspoon ground black pepper

In a large stockpot, combine the tomatoes, onions, garlic, bay leaves, beef stock, chicken stock, parsley sprigs, thyme, tomato paste, and coffee. Then turn the heat to high and bring them to a boil.

Reduce the heat and simmer the soup for approximately 1 hour until the ingredients have reduced in volume by at least 25 percent. Remove the stockpot from the heat.

In a food processor fitted with a metal blade, puree the soup until it's smooth. You may need to do this in batches.

In a large mixing bowl, combine the pureed batches, and stir in the heavy cream, lemon juice, and black pepper. Cover the soup and store it in the refrigerator overnight. When it's time to serve, reheat the soup in a stockpot over medium heat until it's hot throughout but not boiling. Serve immediately.

Butternut Squash Soup

I'D BE delighted to eat this soup all year round. It's a fragrant, pungent combination—a magnificent synthesis of flavors, sweet and savory, with just the right hint of richness. The apples in it, combined with the squash and onions, are a diametrically opposed but balanced delicacy, and the underlying aromas of oregano and rosemary distinguish it among squash soups, which often rely on the accent of milder and more lemony thyme to carry them through. I recommend this soup as a first course for Thanksgiving dinner, or, for that matter, for any lunch or dinner during the fall. I think you'll find it addictive, unexpected, and oh-so-easy.

YIELD: *8 cups, or 6 to 8 servings*

1½ pounds butternut squash	2 teaspoons salt
1½ pounds Red Delicious apples	1 tablespoon dried rosemary
1½ cups diced onions	1 tablespoon dried oregano
2½ cups chicken stock	1 cup heavy cream

Peel and chop the squash into approximately 1½-inch cubes. Peel and core the apples, and chop them into pieces the same size as the squash.

In a medium-sized stockpot over a medium heat, combine the squash, apples, onions, chicken stock, salt, rosemary, and oregano. Bring them to a simmer and cook until the vegetables and apples are tender enough that you can pierce them with a fork, approximately 15 to 20 minutes.

Remove the stockpot from the heat and, in a food processor fitted with a metal blade, puree all the ingredients until they are smooth. You may need to do this in batches.

Pour the pureed vegetables into a medium mixing bowl and stir in the heavy cream. Cover and refrigerate it overnight. When it's time to serve, reheat the soup to a simmer, and serve it hot.

OPPOSITE *So pretty, and all that's missing is a good turn or two in the Cuisinart.*

Sweet Potato "Vichyssoise"

THE WORD *Vichyssoise* sure does sound French, but food cognoscenti know that this beguiling combination, traditionally made with leeks, potatoes, chicken stock, and cream, and served cold, is, in fact, an American invention. It was supposed to have been first served at the Ritz-Carlton Hotel in New York City around the end of World War I by a French chef, Louis Diat, who had been born in the Vichy region of France. According to lore, he remembered a similar hot concoction from his childhood, made of leftover potatoes and cold milk. He developed it as a cold soup and named it accordingly. Here, I use the sweet potato instead of the russet, and the result is delectable and unusual. It sounds and tastes so Southern, and is such a gorgeous color, you may just want to ask your painter to match the hue for your walls!

YIELD: *8 cups, or 6 to 8 servings*

3 tablespoons salted butter	1 cup heavy cream
3 cups diced onions	1 cup buttermilk
3 pounds sweet potatoes	1 teaspoon ground cinnamon
6 cups chicken stock	1 teaspoon ground nutmeg
6 tablespoons sherry	1 teaspoon ground ginger
2½ teaspoons salt	¼ teaspoon ground white pepper

In a medium-sized pot over a high heat bring two quarts of water to a boil.

In a large skillet over a medium heat, melt the butter. When the foaming has subsided, add the onions and sauté them slowly until they are tender and translucent, approximately 8 to 10 minutes. Turn off the heat and reserve.

Peel the sweet potatoes and cut them into one-and-a-half-inch (or so) cubes. To the pot of boiling water, add the sweet potatoes and boil them until they are tender when pierced with a fork, approximately 10 minutes. Drain them in a large colander and reserve them.

In a food processor fitted with a metal blade, puree the sweet potatoes and onions until they are smooth. You may need to do this in batches.

In a medium-sized stockpot, over a medium heat, combine the chicken stock, sherry, salt, heavy cream, buttermilk, cinnamon, nutmeg, ground ginger, and white pepper. Heat them until they just begin to simmer and then turn off the heat.

In a large mixing bowl, combine the pureed sweet potatoes and onions with the liquid mixture and stir well. When the soup has cooled, cover it, refrigerate it overnight, and serve it cold.

Cold Cucumber Soup

THIS WAS a staple at my mother's house. When it was hot outside, which, in Atlanta, it is quite often, there seemed to always be a container of it in our refrigerator. Light, summery, and refreshing, it's very easy to make—no cooking required. And no dried dill, here, please—only fresh. Serve it cold, cold, cold. Best if done the day before, and refrigerated overnight.

YIELD: *8 cups, or 6 to 8 servings*

6 medium cucumbers (about 6 pounds), peeled, seeded, and coarsely chopped
6 green onions, chopped (both the green and white parts)
¼ cup chopped fresh dill
1 tablespoon grated lime zest, minced

4 cups chicken stock
2 tablespoons fresh lime juice
1½ teaspoons salt
½ teaspoon ground black pepper
1 cup buttermilk
1 cup heavy cream
Fresh dill sprigs for garnish

In a food processor fitted with a metal blade, combine the cucumbers, green onions, dill, and lime zest and puree them until they are smooth.

In a large mixing bowl, add the puree of vegetables to the chicken stock, lime juice, salt, pepper, buttermilk, and heavy cream and stir them well to combine. Cover the soup, refrigerate it overnight, and serve it cold, garnished with fresh dill sprigs.

Cold Pea Soup with Mint

THIS SOUP is so easy it practically makes itself. It's ready in five minutes, and so flavorful you can actually serve it the same day, although I think it's better if left to sit in the fridge overnight. Of course, fresh peas would be fantastic here but the frozen ones are great if not. It may be the easiest recipe in the book as there is no hand chopping of any kind involved, and the only skill required is to cut open a bag of frozen, thawed peas and flip the Cuisinart switch.

YIELD: *8 cups, or 6 to 8 servings*

4 cups chicken stock

4 green onions

2 pounds frozen baby peas, thawed but still cold

6 mint leaves, separated from the stems, plus more for garnish

1 teaspoon salt

¼ teaspoon ground black pepper

¼ cup buttermilk

In a food processor fitted with a metal blade, combine all the ingredients and process them until they are smooth. Garnish the soup with fresh mint and serve.

Hot or Cold Red Pepper Soup

PERFECT IN the winter, fantastic in the summer—it's like having two recipes in one. The only trick here is roasting the peppers, and frankly, that's not much of a trick at all. If you are roasting peppers for the Pimiento Cheese recipe on page 22, you might as well go ahead and do some extra ones for this recipe. I am convinced you'll find this so good that it will quickly become a regular part of your culinary repertoire.

YIELD: *8 cups, or 6 to 8 servings*

8 red peppers

½ cup extra-virgin olive oil

1 cup diced onion

2 tablespoons minced garlic

½ cup double-strength tomato paste

2 teaspoons lemon juice

1 teaspoon apple cider vinegar

2½ teaspoons salt

½ teaspoon ground white pepper

2 cups chicken stock

¾ cup heavy cream

½ teaspoon almond extract

2 tablespoons honey

¾ cup plus 2 tablespoons sherry

Preheat the oven to 450°F.

Roast the peppers on a baking sheet in the oven for 15 to 20 minutes, until the skins begin to blacken and blister. When the skins are fully blistered, remove the peppers from the oven, let them cool for 2 to 3 minutes, and then cover them with plastic wrap and let them steam for 15 minutes (the steam will loosen their skin). Remove the plastic wrap and peel the skin. Remove the seeds, chop the peppers coarsely, and reserve them.

In a medium-sized skillet over a medium heat, heat the olive oil until it just starts to move in the pan. Add the onions and sauté them until they just begin to soften, approximately 2 minutes, and then add the garlic. Sauté the onions and garlic for another 2 minutes, and then remove them from the heat.

In a food processor fitted with a metal blade, puree the onions, garlic, and red peppers together until they are smooth. You may need to do this in batches. Transfer the puree to a large mixing bowl.

In a large stockpot over a medium heat, combine the tomato paste, lemon juice, vinegar, salt, white pepper, chicken stock, cream, almond extract, honey, and sherry, and cook them until they just start to simmer. Whisk the ingredients very well to combine thoroughly.

Add the pureed vegetables to the stockpot and turn off the heat. Whisk the soup again to make sure everything is combined. When the soup has cooled, cover it and refrigerate it overnight. Serve it cold or hot.

Cold Avocado Soup

THIS EASY soup is perfect for summer and it is a pretty shade of green. In California the avocados are plentiful and particularly good. I love to serve this as a cold first course for lunch, or in a thermos to keep it cold for a picnic at the Hollywood Bowl.

YIELD: *8 cups, or 6 to 8 servings*

3 ripe avocados, spooned out
   from their skin
1 cup chopped red onion
4 cups chicken stock
½ cup chopped cilantro, plus
   more for garnish

2 tablespoons lemon juice
1½ teaspoons salt
¾ teaspoon ground black pepper
Crème fraîche or sour cream
   for garnish

In a food processor fitted with a metal blade, puree the avocados, onions, and chicken stock until they are smooth.

In a large mixing bowl, combine the pureed vegetables and add the cilantro, lemon juice, salt, and pepper. Stir the soup well to combine thoroughly.

Garnish with a dollop of crème fraîche or sour cream, and additional chopped cilantro, and serve it immediately.

It's arranged so beautifully on the plate,

you just know someone's fingers have been all over it!

JULIA CHILD

3

Salads

The salad can be a first or main course, a side dish or an after-course. There is no end to the creativity one can employ with salads. They are perfect for right-brained creative people who love to experiment, and they should use my recipes here for inspiration. Please let me know the results. If you are not a culinary experimenter, however, follow these recipes to the letter (please note that I have even included what I consider to be the correct amount of dressing per salad) and you'll have success each time. Every one of these recipes is easy, and although some of them have more steps than others, unlike braising, baking, roasting, or sautéing, these dishes require few to zero in the culinary skills department.

OPPOSITE *Chilled Champagne seems right with Lobster Salad Remoulade (page 77).*

Broccoli Slaw

A COLE SLAW that is pretty to look at. Sign me up. As a plus, it's not sweet either, a characteristic I abhor in more traditional slaws. This colorful, fresh, crunchy interpretation is a perfect complement to basic fried chicken, and more upscale fare too. I serve it at my dinner the night before the Oscars every year, a somewhat healthy alternative to the soul food I put on the rest of the buffet. More on this party later. This slaw is really gorgeous in a glass bowl as it's richly toned, and full of inviting texture.

YIELD: *8 cups, or 6 to 8 servings*

SLAW
2 cups blanched (see instructions) fresh broccoli, stems and florets (approximately one head with stems), chopped
2 cups medium-diced green cabbage
2 cups finely sliced red cabbage
¾ cup diced yellow bell peppers
¼ cup minced shallots
½ cup chopped fresh dill
¾ teaspoon salt
¾ teaspoon ground black pepper

YIELD: *1½ cups*

DRESSING
¾ cup Perfect Homemade Mayonnaise (page 126), or store-bought
½ cup sour cream
¾ teaspoon lemon juice
¾ teaspoon salt
¼ teaspoon ground black pepper
1½ tablespoons Dijon mustard

Bring a medium pot of water to a boil over high heat and add 1 teaspoon of salt per each quart (4 cups) of water. Place 2 cups ice cubes in a large bowl.

Add the broccoli to the salted boiling water and blanch it for 1 minute exactly, until it turns bright green. Drain the broccoli in a colander.

Quickly place the broccoli in the bowl with the ice cubes to discontinue further cooking.

When it is cool, drain and dry the broccoli, and then chop it, both florets and stems.

In a large mixing bowl, combine the green and red cabbages, yellow peppers, shallots, dill, salt, and pepper. Add the broccoli. Add 1 cup of the dressing, stir the slaw very well, cover it, and refrigerate it overnight. The next day, you may need to add the remaining ½ cup of dressing for moisture before serving the slaw cold.

Spinach, Red Onion, Prosciutto, and Blue Cheese Salad with Red Wine Vinaigrette

THIS IS, hands down, my favorite of all salads. I think it will be yours, too. The crispness of the spinach combined with the sharp prosciutto and blue cheese becomes poetry when married with the red wine vinaigrette and the tang of the onions. I often serve it at buffets, as it goes with just about anything, and wholeheartedly suggest that you add grilled chicken to it for a delicious main course at lunch.

YIELD: *4 to 6 servings*

2 ounces prosciutto (about 4 thin slices)
½ pound fresh spinach, cleaned
1 tablespoon (½ ounce) crumbled blue cheese

1 ounce shaved red onion, approximately 3 tablespoons
6 tablespoons Red Wine Vinaigrette (page 140)

Preheat the oven to 400°F.

Place the prosciutto on a heavy baking sheet and bake it for 8 minutes, until it has curled and is crisp. Remove the prosciutto from the oven and, when it's cool, crumble it in your hand into pieces.

In a medium-sized salad bowl, combine the spinach, prosciutto, blue cheese, and red onions.

When it's time to serve the salad, toss it with the red wine vinaigrette at least sixteen times, so that all leaves are fully coated with the dressing, and serve.

Avocado, Grapefruit, and Macadamia Nut Salad with Manchego Cheese and Poppyseed Vinaigrette

I WANT to ask you to join me on a trip: Imagine us together in Dallas, Texas, circa 1960. Neiman-Marcus is the center of the elegant universe, and, of course, it has the best restaurant in town. I think we should go there for lunch. Helen Corbitt is there, presiding over her culinary empire, and, boy, is she famous! Sought after for her unusual combinations, upscale sensibility, and all-around amazing efforts, Stanley Marcus, one of the world's most brilliant merchants, courted her for years before she finally joined the Neiman's team. The fact that she is a Yankee, born and bred in New York City, is excused, because she taught Texans how to really eat.

Corbitt (1906–1978) spent forty years in Texas in the food business catering to Texas's burgeoning carriage trade and becoming renowned around the

United States among Neiman's customers and other enthusiasts for posh and delicious food. She wrote more books than the law should allow. One of her most famous recipes was for poppyseed vinaigrette, which she served over gorgeous Texas ruby red grapefruits in winter. I reexamined this classic, and found that the original recipe was far too sweet for today's tastes, but the idea was captivating and current. Below you'll find an updated version of the Corbitt classic, and one that I serve usually on New Year's night because that's just about the right time for those beautiful fruits to reach their full potential.

(continued on page 72)

This Neiman-Marcus model circa 1950 looks like she could use a visit to Helen Corbitt's restaurant in the store, The Zodiac Room.

(continued from page 70)

YIELD: *4 to 6 servings*

1 head Bibb (these days they call it "butter") lettuce

1 large Texas ruby red grapefruit

3 tablespoons roasted whole macadamia nuts

2 tablespoons grated or diced Manchego cheese

1 medium avocado

Salt and freshly ground black pepper

6 tablespoons poppyseed vinaigrette (recipe follows)

Wash and thoroughly dry the lettuce. Break the leaves into pieces. Peel and section the grapefruit.

Mix the lettuce, macadamia nuts, and cheese in a large bowl, then add salt and pepper to taste.

Just before serving, so that they don't turn brown, peel the avocado, cut it into large chunks, and add it to the salad bowl.

Add the poppyseed vinaigrette and toss the salad at least sixteen times. Add the grapefruit sections on top, so as not to break the sections, drizzle them with a bit more of the vinaigrette, and serve.

Poppyseed Vinaigrette

YIELD: *4 cups*

1 cup red wine vinegar

3 tablespoons poppy seeds

3 tablespoons minced red onion

3 tablespoons minced garlic

2 tablespoons dry mustard

1 tablespoon salt

½ cup sugar

1 teaspoon ground black pepper

3 cups vegetable oil

In a medium-sized mixing bowl combine the vinegar, poppy seeds, red onion, garlic, mustard, salt, sugar, and pepper. Add the vegetable oil slowly in droplets, whisking constantly to make the perfect emulsion.

Quail Salad with Lentil Vinaigrette and Goat Cheese Crostini

I AM going to drop a name. It may not be one that you know, but it's one you sure should. Edna Lewis (1916–2006) was widely recognized as one of the leading authorities on indigenous Southern cooking, and I was lucky enough to have known her. She had an amazing life. The great-granddaughter of a slave in Virginia, Lewis became the chef at New York's famous celebrity haunt Café Nicholson, tucked away near the Fifty-ninth Street bridge, and frequented by such luminaries of its midcentury heyday as William Faulkner, Richard Avedon, and Tennessee Williams. She was discovered by Judith Jones, the legendary Knopf editor who also discovered Julia Child, and Lewis wrote many books during her life. By the

Edna Lewis was a guest chef at The Patio by the River in 1992.

time I knew her in the early 1990s she was roundly considered to be the "Julia Child of Southern Cooking." She came to The Patio by the River as a guest chef several times, and declared our quail salad to be the best one she'd ever had. Strong talk from Miss Edna, and I'll take it! She ordered it again and again.

YIELD: *6 servings*

18 semi-boneless quails
(allow 3 quails per person
as they are small)
Salt and coarsely ground black
pepper

2½ cups Lentil Vinaigrette, divided
(recipe follows)
½ to ¾ pounds mixed mesclun greens
Goat Cheese Crostini (page 76)
Fresh chopped parsley for garnish

Season both sides of the quails generously with salt and pepper. In a deep baking dish, arrange the quails neatly and pour 1¾ cups of the lentil vinaigrette

(continued on page 75)

(continued from page 73)

over the quail. Mix the quail and the vinaigrette thoroughly and then cover them and let them marinate overnight in the refrigerator.

On a very hot grill or grill pan over a very high heat, grill the quail until they are rare or medium rare, crusty on the outside but still moist on the inside. This will take only a couple of minutes per side. Reserve them and let them cool slightly.

In a large salad bowl, dress the greens with the remaining ½ cup of the lentil vinaigrette, tossing at least sixteen times to fully coat the leaves. For presentation, arrange the quails neatly on the top of the bed of greens, and garnish the salad with goat cheese crostini. Pour another couple of tablespoons of the lentil vinaigrette over the top of the quails, garnish the quails with fresh chopped parsley, and serve.

Lentil Vinaigrette

Let's talk about quail salad. This delicious vinaigrette was originally inspired by a French recipe from the Dordogne region of France where my mother's house is. Dordogne is the capital of truffles, foie gras, cassoulet, lentils, and walnuts. From walnuts come walnut oil, and then throw in some lentils, chicken stock, garlic, and parsley, *et alia,* and why not, just why not, toss it over quail—I am sure you get the logic even if I don't! It's just one of those things. Here's my guarantee: grill up those baby semi-boneless quails and throw this deliciousness on, and if the logic has heretofore eluded you, it won't anymore!

YIELD: *3½ cups*

½ cup dry lentils, cooked according to package directions to yield approximately 1¼ cups cooked lentils

¼ cup red wine vinegar

1 tablespoon chopped parsley

2 tablespoons lemon juice

2 teaspoons minced garlic

2⅛ teaspoons salt

¼ teaspoon freshly ground black pepper

1 cup extra-virgin olive oil

1 cup walnut oil

½ cup chicken stock

¼ cup coarsely chopped toasted walnuts

(continued on next page)

In the bowl of a food processor fitted with a metal blade, puree the lentils, vinegar, parsley, lemon juice, garlic, salt, and pepper.

While the machine is running, add the oils by droplets to the lentil mixture. Then add the chicken stock. An emulsion will form when all the liquid has been added.

Pour the vinaigrette into a medium bowl and stir in the chopped walnuts. Serve over the grilled quail.

Goat Cheese Crostini

YIELD: *About 18 crostini*

½ stick (4 tablespoons) salted butter, melted

1 French baguette, crusty on the outside, yet soft in the inside (tough, hard bread will make crostini you could break a tooth on)

4 to 6 ounces goat cheese, softened

Preheat the oven to 325°F.

In a heavy small saucepan over medium heat, melt the butter. Slice the baguette into ½-inch slices, and place the slices on a heavy baking sheet. Put the baking sheet in the oven, and bake it for 12 minutes exactly.

Flip the slices over and, with a pastry brush, evenly "paint" the untoasted side with the melted butter. Put the baking sheet back in the oven, and bake the crostini for another 18 minutes, until they are brown and thoroughly dried out.

Remove them from the oven, and let them cool before spreading the goat cheese on top. These can be served either slightly warm or cool.

Lobster Salad Remoulade

THERE IS a well-known catering shop on Long Island between Southampton and East Hampton that is famous for its lobster salad. It's very good (please note: very good means not as good as this one) but mostly it is renowned for its price. In the flush years before the economy tanked, they charged as much as $125.00 per pound for their lobster salad. Now they may charge as much as 30 percent less. Detractors say the fluctuating price is an economic bellwether, and I must say, I agree.

I have borrowed my favorite New Orleans remoulade to bind this delicious and colorful salad that's just perfect for a summer lunch or first course on a special summer night. And when I think of New Orleans remoulade, I think of Galatoire's restaurant. Serve it over a bed of greens with crostini, and you'll have yet another sure-fire hit.

YIELD: *6 to 8 servings*

2 tablespoons salted butter
2 pounds lobster meat, peeled,
    and chopped into chunks
1 medium onion, diced
3 stalks celery, chopped
2 slices very crisp cooked bacon,
    chopped
¾ cup Remoulade Sauce
    (recipe follows)

1 large tomato, diced
2 tablespoons Dijon mustard
1 tablespoon lemon juice
¾ teaspoon salt
½ teaspoon freshly ground
    black pepper
Remoulade Sauce (recipe follows)

In a large skillet over a medium heat, melt the butter. When the foaming has subsided, add the lobster and sauté it for only a couple of minutes, until the butter fully covers it. Remove it from the heat, set it aside, and let it cool.

In a large bowl, combine the lobster with the onion, celery, bacon, remoulade sauce, tomato, Dijon mustard, lemon juice, salt, and pepper, and cover it. Refrigerate the lobster salad overnight before serving. Serve it cold on a bed of lettuce, with avocados, tomatoes, or corn on the cob.

Remoulade Sauce

This sauce is the cousin of Gribiche (page 129), with a thicker, more mayonnaise-like consistency. I think of New Orleans whenever I hear the word, and love it with shrimp, scallops, lobster, and oysters. Imagine a Cobb salad with seafood instead of chicken, and a good remoulade should never be too far away.

YIELD: *A little more than 1 cup*

¾ cup mayonnaise, homemade
    (page 126) or store-bought
¼ cup crème fraîche
1 garlic clove, minced
2 tablespoons Dijon mustard
¾ teaspoon dry mustard

1 tablespoon finely minced
    Italian parsley
1 teaspoon dried tarragon
1 teaspoon anchovy paste
1½ teaspoons chopped capers

In a small mixing bowl combine all the ingredients and stir, cover the bowl, and refrigerate it for at least 2 hours, or preferably overnight, and serve.

Crab Salad with Bloody Mary Aspic

FEW THINGS conjure as many memories in the South as tomato aspic. It is a staple at Southern gatherings: weddings, lunches, funerals, and what-all. Like many recipes in this book, it's a dish we just don't hear about so much anymore. Too bad, because it's great. Here, it serves as a steady and happy partner to the cold and elegant crabmeat salad. Its tartness provides a fantastic flavor *contrapunto* to the dill in the vinaigrette of the crab. This is so pretty when it's unmolded that you will look like the genius culinary artisan that you are, or aspire to be!

YIELD: *6 to 8 servings*

2 pounds jumbo lump crabmeat, picked through and cleaned
1 cup vegetable oil
¼ cup apple cider vinegar
1½ cups finely chopped onions

2 teaspoons salt
¾ teaspoon ground white pepper
2¼ teaspoons dried dill
1 cup Gravlax Sauce (page 83)
Fresh chopped dill for garnish

In a large mixing bowl, combine all the ingredients and mix them well, but gently, so as not to break the lumps of crabmeat up too much. Cover, and refrigerate the salad overnight.

Drain it, and serve it in the middle of a mold of Bloody Mary Aspic (page 82) with Parmesan Tuiles (page 15).

Bloody Mary Aspic

Please note, this recipe has two ingredients lists because there are two distinct stages in the process for making this updated classic.

YIELD: *One 4-cup mold, 6 to 8 servings*

4 cups tomato juice

2 tablespoons lemon juice

½ medium onion, sliced

2 bay leaves

½ cup diced celery

½ cup chopped carrots

2 tablespoons minced fresh ginger

1 tablespoon fresh horseradish, drained

In a 2-quart saucepan over a medium heat, bring all the ingredients above to a simmer, and then reduce the heat to low. Let the ingredients steep for 30 minutes on low heat.

Strain the mixture through a sieve so that you have only liquid remaining. Discard all the solids.

---

2 tablespoons finely minced onion

½ cup diced celery

½ cup diced carrots

1½ teaspoons salt

1 teaspoon ground black pepper

1 tablespoons sugar

2 tablespoons unflavored gelatin

½ cup apple cider vinegar

Fresh Bibb lettuce for garnish

To the strained liquid, add the onions, celery, carrots, salt, ground black pepper, and sugar. Mix everything well and let it cool fully.

Dissolve the gelatin into the vinegar, and add it all to the tomato juice mixture, and stir it gently. Set the liquid in a 4-cup mold—for this I love to use a Bundt pan. Chill it overnight to set.

Unmold the aspic onto a serving platter and garnish it with fresh lettuce. In the middle of the unmolded aspic, pile the crabmeat salad and garnish it with fresh chopped dill, and then serve it cold.

Gravlax Sauce

I call this Gravlax Sauce because at The Patio by the River we served it on house-cured salmon on a bed of baby greens, which we offered for a first course at lunch or dinner. (Watch for that recipe in another book.) This sauce is an excellent lighter mayonnaise, one that I use as an ingredient in the Crab Salad (page 80) and one you should experiment with whenever you need just that perfect dose of extra flavor.

YIELD: *about 2 cups, so you'll have a bit left over*
if this is to be used in the Crab Salad

1½ cups Perfect Homemade
   Mayonnaise (page 126)
1 cup sour cream
3 tablespoons Dijon mustard

1½ teaspoons lemon juice
½ teaspoon ground white pepper
¾ teaspoon salt

Mix all the ingredients together in a medium bowl.

My Chicken Salad

IN THE hors d'oeuvres chapter, you met this one's cousin, the Basil-Parmesan Chicken Salad (page 37). Here's a bit of a different take, a theme and variations exercise. I absolutely love chicken salad, and as good as these two recipes are—and believe me, they are really good—there are many others in the world that are, too. In my opinion, there can simply never be too much chicken salad.

This is perfect as a light lunch, or on a cucumber round as a passed cold summer hors d'oeuvre. It seems I just can't stay away from pecans, and the roasting of them for this dish brings a subtle but nutty flavor that beautifully complements the lightness the lemon juice imparts. And the fresh tarragon provides an aromatic, slightly bittersweet flavor to the finish.

YIELD: *4 to 6 servings*

2 pounds cooked chicken (page 7), or just buy a rotisserie chicken from your local store

¼ cup diced celery

¼ cup diced yellow or white onions

¾ cup Perfect Homemade Mayonnaise (page 126)

1 tablespoon plus 1½ teaspoons lemon juice

½ teaspoon salt

¼ teaspoon ground black pepper

¼ cup chopped roasted pecans

2 tablespoons chopped tarragon

"Pull" the chicken so that it becomes shredded. In a large mixing bowl, combine all the ingredients.

In a food processor fitted with a metal blade, pulse the mixture to your desired consistency or simply keep it as it is. Serve the salad with Parmesan Tuiles (page 15) over a bed of lettuce.

OPPOSITE *Mark Tydell has a steady hand with My Chicken Salad and Bloody Mary Aspic (page 82).*

Salmon Salad

ANOTHER TAKE on salmon tartare (page 24)! For this delicious salad, I am going to insist on the delicacy of homemade mayonnaise because, as good as the commercial stuff can be, the homemade stuff is always better. The delicate salmon flavor is enhanced by the shallots, dill, lemon, and pepper. This salad is destined to become a classic, and has, in my house, replaced the ubiquitous tuna salad that we all love.

YIELD: *4 to 6 servings*

¼ cup chopped celery

¼ cup chopped shallots

2 tablespoons chopped fresh dill

2 tablespoons lemon juice

½ cup Perfect Homemade
   Mayonnaise (page 126)

2 tablespoons crème fraîche

1 tablespoon Dijon mustard

½ teaspoon salt

⅛ teaspoon ground black pepper

2 pounds cooked salmon

Lettuce for serving

In a large mixing bowl, combine the celery, shallots, dill, lemon juice, mayonnaise, crème fraîche, Dijon mustard, salt, and pepper together and mix them well. Add the salmon whole and stir the salad together. The salmon will break up very easily, so there is no need to chop. Serve the salad cold over a bed of lettuce.

OPPOSITE *I keep many cookbooks handy in the kitchen because I refer to them so often.*

Pear Salad with Parmesan and Hazelnuts

THIS MAY be the ultimate salad. It's a symphony of savory and sweet; fresh and crunchy from the lettuce, nutty from the hazels, cheesy (and not in the bad way) from the Parmesan, and sweet from the poached pear. This masterpiece looks complicated, but in fact, is not. When it's not salad time, I love to serve these poached pears with vanilla ice cream and chocolate sauce, but we'll save that for another book!

YIELD: *8 servings*

1 recipe Perfect Poached Pears
  (page 318)
1 head red leaf lettuce
¼ cup shredded Parmesan cheese
2 tablespoons chopped hazelnuts
¼ cup chopped parsley

½ cup Dijon Mustard Vinaigrette
  (page 141)
¼ cup poaching liquid from
  Perfect Poached Pears recipe

Wash and thoroughly dry the lettuce. In a large salad bowl, break up the lettuce, and add the Parmesan, hazelnuts, and parsley. Add the mustard vinaigrette and poaching liquid and toss at least sixteen times so all the leaves are covered. Serve it cold.

Rice Salad

THIS COLORFUL side dish served cold can easily step into the main role with the simple addition of some grilled chicken or tuna at lunchtime. There are versions of this dish served throughout Europe, especially in Spain, where it seems they are always serving rice.

YIELD: *6 to 8 servings*

2 cups cooked rice

1 tablespoon chopped green onions

1 tablespoon diced red bell pepper

1 tablespoon diced yellow bell pepper

2 tablespoons minced onion

3 tablespoons chopped parsley

2 tablespoons diced carrots

2 tablespoons diced celery

½ teaspoon salt

3 tablespoons Dijon Mustard Vinaigrette (page 141)

2 teaspoons lemon juice

½ teaspoon minced garlic

In a medium-sized mixing bowl, combine all the ingredients and mix them well. Cover the salad and chill it overnight, or for at least 4 hours, so that the flavors come together.

OPPOSITE *Adding the Dijon Mustard Vinaigrette (page 141) to the Rice Salad*

4

Eggs, and Cheese, and Grits, and Quiche!

The age-old adage for proper entertaining, when it comes to first courses, goes something like this: "Eggs for lunch, soup for dinner." I have reinterpreted this idea a bit, and often serve things like scrambled eggs with caviar or smoked salmon as a first course for dinner, much to the delight of my guests. I absolutely love eggs in any fashion, and have had such fun assembling these favorite recipes, combined with some very notable grits and quiche recipes, which I refer to as "tarts" in these pages as benign acquiescence to the "Real Men Don't Eat Quiche" pop-culture admonition from the seventies. I probably wouldn't serve a Four Cheese Soufflé (page 103) or Soufflé "Suissesse" (page 106) as a first course for dinner, as somehow these two seem much more lusciously lunchlike, or even that dreaded word *brunchlike*, but go right ahead with the Salmon Soufflé (page 113), Spinach Soufflé (page 109), Red

OPPOSITE *This Four Cheese Soufflé (page 103) bakes in about thirty minutes.*

Pepper (page 115) or Mushroom Tarts (page 117), or Bill Blass's famous Sour Cream Soufflé (page 111), which, incidentally, he served as a main dish for lunch with a simple green salad. The cheese grits in these pages are perfect as side dishes for breakfast, lunch, and dinner, and Brooke's "Confetti" Grits (page 119) are a show-stopper on just about any buffet. Please note that egg cookery is specific and requires attention; I'm not saying that it's difficult, and I am very fanatical on times and textures, it's just that it requires precision. An overcooked egg is something awful, indeed.

This chapter demystifies the process of making soufflés. If you're still not comfortable with the idea, or question your own abilities, please immediately make the Soufflé "Suissesse" (page 106), a twice-baked, reengineered version of the Four Cheese Soufflé (page 103), which requires no urgency in timing. It can be fully done ahead of time, and there is no worry about having it fall.

French Scrambled Eggs with Caviar

THIS IS special occasion food. American paddlefish roe is perfect for this dish, but you can always substitute smoked salmon or lightly poached shrimp for the caviar and you'll still have a winner. Serve this as a first course at dinner or a main course at lunch, but make sure the main course is a "pull-back." I'll explain this later, but an unpretentious meatloaf with green peas or a really good homemade chicken pot pie will help you balance the menu and show your guests that you're comfortable enough in your own skin to serve good simple food, rather than trying to impress them with how fancy you are!

YIELD: *4 servings*

2 tablespoons salted butter
8 eggs
2 tablespoons crème fraîche
⅛ teaspoon salt
Coarsely ground black pepper

1 tablespoon snipped chives for garnish
A dollop of sour cream for garnish
2 ounces caviar, the best quality your pocketbook allows

In a double boiler over a medium-low heat, melt the butter.

In a large mixing bowl, whisk together the eggs, crème fraîche, salt, and pepper. Strain them through a fine sieve.

When the butter is fully melted and still foaming, pour the egg mixture into the double boiler. Stir the eggs with a wooden spoon constantly until soft curds form. This will take a while—15 or 20 minutes—but be patient because the consistency is unparalleled. These luxurious eggs are like nothing you've ever tasted in America, yet have been staples in French households for generations. Remove soft scrambled eggs to a heated soufflé dish or serving platter, garnish with the snipped chives, sour cream, and caviar, and serve.

Scrambled Eggs with Smoked Salmon

Follow the same process as for the preceding recipe, but substitute the best-quality smoked salmon for the caviar.

Eggs Sardou

FOR TWO centuries New Orleans has been known as a town of innovative Creole-French cuisine, for quality in its kitchens, and for unprecedented and exacting culinary standards. It was the food capital of America long before the first American foodie drew his or her first breath. My favorite restaurant there is Galatoire's, and I adapt here one of their time-honored festive lunch dishes. Here's the glory: the spinach-artichoke mixture can be done ahead of time, frozen, and heated up in your microwave when it's time for these easy, impressive eggs.

YIELD: *6 servings*

6 eggs

3 English muffins, split and toasted

12 tablespoons Creamed Spinach with Artichokes (page 170), warmed

One recipe Perfect Hollandaise Sauce (page 131)

Lightly poach the eggs in salted water and reserve.

On each of 6 toasted English muffin halves, place 2 tablespoons of the creamed spinach and artichokes, 1 poached egg, and 2 tablespoons of the hollandaise sauce. Serve immediately.

FOLLOWING SPREAD *Eggs Sardou is a more colorful cousin of eggs Benedict.*

Four Cheese Soufflé

AT MOST cooking schools, the soufflé is not usually taught until at least the second week or so. In other words, this technique is rudimentary, but not quite as rudimentary as trussing a chicken or holding a knife and chopping onions. This one is based on the classic recipe from Le Cordon Bleu, which you may know better as the one that Julia Child published in her 1961 seminal work, *Mastering the Art of French Cooking, Volume 1*. With absolutely no disrespect meant for Miss Julia—I consider her the ultimate luminary, a goddess, a magician, a taskmaster, and a supreme being in every way—I find her basic cheese soufflé is merely passable, not really very good, and certainly not great. Forgive me. I have added some different cheeses here and have punched up the flavors with cayenne pepper and mustard. I would hope that Julia would be very pleased with the result. It's at once luscious and light, awe-inspiring and easy, formal yet accessible. The four cheeses are in harmony, virtually indistinguishable one from another so much so that I feel their combination could be marketed as a completely new cheese all its own. There are lots of steps, but all of them are easy and clearly defined.

YIELD: *4 to 6 servings*

3 tablespoons salted butter, plus more for the soufflé dish

4 tablespoons grated Parmesan cheese, divided

3 tablespoons flour

1 cup milk

¾ teaspoon salt, plus a pinch, divided

½ teaspoon ground white pepper

¼ teaspoon nutmeg

¼ teaspoon cayenne pepper

1 teaspoon minced garlic

6 egg yolks

½ cup grated sharp Cheddar cheese, firmly packed

½ cup grated Gruyère cheese, firmly packed

½ cup crumbled blue cheese

1 tablespoon Dijon mustard

1 teaspoon lemon juice

1 tablespoon white wine

8 egg whites

(continued on next page)

OPPOSITE *Don't be discouraged, because all soufflés deflate a bit, but they are still luscious on the inside.*

(continued from previous page)

Preheat the oven to 400°F. Butter a 6-cup soufflé dish or two 4-cup soufflé dishes. The smaller the dish, the higher the soufflé will rise. Add 2 tablespoons of the Parmesan cheese and shake the buttered dishes to coat them with the Parmesan.

In a heavy skillet over medium heat, melt the butter and add the flour to make a roux. Stir it with a wooden spoon or a rubber spatula until it is fully cooked through but not brown. This will take 3 to 4 minutes.

In a heavy pot over medium-high heat, heat the milk until it is scalding but not boiling. Add ¾ teaspoon of the salt, the white pepper, nutmeg, cayenne pepper, and garlic, and stir thoroughly to combine these ingredients with the milk.

Add the roux to the milk and whisk it vigorously to fully combine so there are no lumpy bits of roux in the milk. Bring the mixture to a boil and then remove it from the heat. It will have thickened considerably.

Let the mixture cool for 5 to 10 minutes and pour it into a medium mixing bowl.

Stir in the egg yolks, one by one, and then the remaining 2 tablespoons of Parmesan, Cheddar, Gruyère, and blue cheeses, and the mustard, lemon juice, and white wine.

In the bowl of a large electric stand mixer fitted with the whisk attachment, beat the egg whites with a pinch of salt until they stand in soft peaks. Add ⅓ of the whipped egg whites to the mixing bowl and stir it well to lighten the mixture. Fold in the remaining egg whites.

Reduce the oven temperature to 350°F.

Pour the soufflé mixture gently into the prepared soufflé dish so as not to deflate the egg whites, and bake it for 25 to 30 minutes until it has risen. Serve it immediately.

NOTE I love to undercook soufflés because the underdone part in the middle makes its own sauce for the soufflé and you don't need a separate sauce. That is my preference, but do it however you feel most comfortable.

Soufflé "Vendôme"

PLACE VENDÔME, Paris: home of the Hotel Ritz, Charvet, JAR, and all of the poshest of the posh. It just doesn't get any fancier than this. How ironic that the Soufflé "Vendôme," a cheese soufflé with poached eggs, is as easy as it is. Just make the Four Cheese Soufflé (page 103), and after you butter the soufflé dishes and before putting the soufflé mixture in for baking, line the bottom of the dish with 4 to 6 lightly poached eggs, pour the soufflé mix over the top, and then bake it for 25 to 30 minutes. There will be a surprise at the bottom, a luxurious treasure hunt that will marvel pros and amateurs alike, and is an excellent lunch dish, for a change.

This brace of an elegant lantern on Place Vendôme displays the monogram of Louis XIV.

Soufflé "Suissesse"

A twice-baked cheese soufflé with tomato sauce

PURE MAGIC! It's an excellent solution for those of you who might be intimidated by the pressure of timing a regular soufflé. This is the one to try. Everything can be done ahead and reheated, and the result is extraordinary. Please notice that the chemistry is a bit different from that of the Four Cheese Soufflé, and it needs to be that way because of the second baking.

YIELD: *6 to 8 servings*

3 tablespoons salted butter, plus
    more for the souflé dish

4 tablespoons Parmesan cheese,
    divided

3 tablespoons flour

¾ cup milk

1 teaspoon salt, plus a pinch, divided

½ teaspoon white pepper

¼ teaspoon nutmeg

¼ teaspoon cayenne pepper

1 teaspoon minced garlic

¾ cup heavy cream

8 egg yolks

½ cup grated sharp Cheddar
    cheese, firmly packed

½ cup grated Gruyère cheese,
    firmly packed

½ cup crumbled blue cheese

1 tablespoon Dijon mustard

1 teaspoon lemon juice

6 egg whites

Preheat the oven to 400°F. Butter a 6-cup soufflé dish or two 4-cup soufflé dishes. The smaller the dish, the higher the soufflé will rise. Add 2 tablespoons of the Parmesan cheese and shake the buttered dishes to coat them with it.

Melt the butter in a heavy skillet over medium heat and add the flour to make a roux. Stir it with a wooden spoon or a rubber spatula until it is fully cooked through but not brown. This will take 3 to 4 minutes.

Heat the milk in a heavy pot over a medium-high heat until it is scalding but not boiling. Add the 1 teaspoon of the salt, white pepper, nutmeg, cayenne pepper, and garlic, and stir to thoroughly combine these ingredients with the milk.

Add the roux to the milk and whisk it vigorously to fully combine so there are no lumpy bits of roux in the milk. Bring the mixture to a boil and then remove it from the heat. It will have thickened considerably.

Let the mixture cool for 5 to 10 minutes and pour it into a medium mixing bowl. Stir in the egg yolks, one by one, and then the remaining 2 tablespoons of Parmesan, the Cheddar, Gruyère, blue cheeses, mustard, and lemon juice.

In the bowl of a large electric stand mixer fitted with the whisk attachment, beat the egg whites with a pinch of salt until they stand in soft peaks. Add ⅓ of the whipped egg whites to the mixing bowl and stir it well to lighten the mixture. Fold in the remaining egg whites.

Reduce the oven temperature to 350°F.

Pour the soufflé mixture gently into the prepared soufflé dish so as not to deflate the egg whites, and bake it for 30 to 35 minutes until it is fully set. Let it cool for 20 minutes. Around the perimeter of the dish, loosen the edges with the dull side of a knife.

Invert the soufflé onto an ovenproof baking dish or serving platter for rebaking, and let it cool completely. (This may be done up to several days ahead of time.)

When it's time to serve the soufflé, preheat the oven to 450°F. Generously pour all of the tomato sauce over the top of the inverted soufflé. There will be a puddle of sauce. Bake it again for 15 to 20 minutes, until the soufflé has puffed again and is brown and bubbling. Serve immediately.

Tomato Sauce for Soufflé "Suissesse"

YIELD: *Exactly enough to cover the Soufflé for the gratin*

3 large tomatoes, peeled, seeded, and diced

1½ cups heavy cream

1 cup white wine

1 cup grated Parmesan cheese, firmly packed

2 teaspoons dried tarragon

1 tablespoon tomato paste

1 teaspoon lemon juice

1 teaspoon salt

¼ teaspoon white pepper

¼ teaspoon cracked black pepper

In a heavy saucepan over medium-high heat, combine all the ingredients, except the Parmesan cheese, and bring them to a boil for 20 minutes. Remove the sauce from the heat and let it cool for about 5 minutes. Stir in the Parmesan cheese, and pour the sauce over the inverted soufflé.

Spinach Soufflé

ALTHOUGH THERE is no question that fresh spinach is better here, you may make your life easier and use frozen. There, I've said it. Just don't quote me.

This colorful treat is an excellent first course for dinner. Throw a bit of smoked salmon or prosciutto on top, and you have an unusual main dish for lunch that is lighter, for those of us who worry about these things, than the splurge of a cheese soufflé, but that is certainly no less appetizing.

YIELD: *4 to 6 servings*

5 tablespoons salted butter, plus
    more for the soufflé dish, divided
6 tablespoons Parmesan cheese
2 pounds spinach
1½ teaspoons salt, plus a pinch,
    divided
¼ teaspoon black pepper
1 cup half-and-half
½ teaspoon white pepper

1 teaspoon minced garlic
½ teaspoon nutmeg
3 tablespoons flour
6 egg yolks
1 cup grated Gruyère cheese,
    firmly packed
1 tablespoon Dijon mustard
2 teaspoons dry vermouth
8 egg whites

(continued on next page)

OPPOSITE *Add ⅓ of the whipped egg whites to the mixing bowl and stir it well to lighten the mixture.* ABOVE, LEFT *Add the remaining egg whites.* ABOVE, RIGHT *Fold them in.*

Red Pepper Tart

THIS QUICHE can be served warm or cold, at any time of the year, as a main or first course, or cut into pieces as an easy hors d'oeuvre.

NOTE You will see in the photographs the way I use cookie cutters to shape this tart into perfect-size hors d'oeuvres. The advantage of making this tart in baking pans rather than pie pans allows for much easier preparation and presentation.

YIELD: *8 to 10 servings*

8 large red bell peppers
5 whole eggs
5 egg yolks
1 cup heavy cream
1 tablespoon lemon juice
½ cup grated Gruyère cheese,
    firmly packed
3 tablespoons chopped chives

2 teaspoons chicken stock base
1 teaspoon sugar
½ cup grated Parmesan cheese
2 tablespoons salted butter, melted
1¼ teaspoon salt
¼ teaspoon ground black pepper
Basic Pâte Brisée (page 268)

(continued on next page)

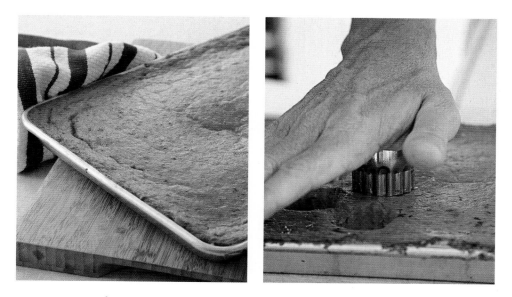

ABOVE, LEFT *This Red Pepper Tart is in a 9 × 13-inch baking pan, also known as a quarter-sheet pan.* ABOVE, RIGHT *Use whatever size cookie cutter you want—smaller for passed hors d'oeuvres or larger for a first or main course.*

(continued from previous page)

Preheat the oven to 450°F.

Roast the peppers on a baking sheet in the oven for 15 to 20 minutes, until the skins begin to blacken and blister. When the skins are fully blistered, remove the peppers from the oven, let them cool for 2 to 3 minutes, and then cover them with plastic wrap and let them steam for 15 minutes (the steam will loosen their skin). Remove the plastic wrap and peel the skin. Chop the peppers in half, discard the seeds, and dice the remaining pepper strips.

Let the peppers drain in a colander for at least 15 minutes, tossing them occasionally, to get out all of the extra water.

In a food processor fitted with a metal blade, puree the peppers until they are smooth. The pureed peppers should measure about 4 cups.

In a large mixing bowl, whisk together the eggs, egg yolks, cream, lemon juice, Gruyère, chives, chicken stock base, sugar, Parmesan, melted butter, salt, and black pepper until they are well blended. Stir in the pepper puree until it is fully combined. This is gorgeous!

Turn the oven down to 325°F.

Pour the mixture into the prebaked 9 × 13-inch tart shell and bake for 25 to 30 minutes, until it is slightly firm. Remove it from the oven and let it cool for at least 15 minutes before slicing it into whatever size pieces you desire. Serve it warm or cold.

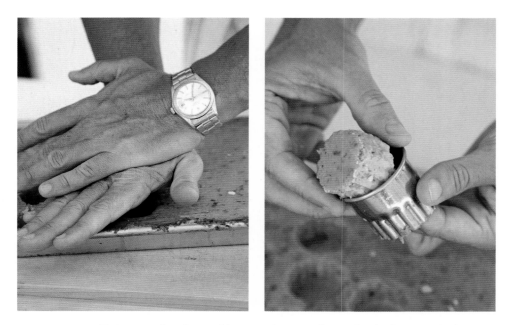

ABOVE, LEFT *Make sure that the cookie cutter is pressed completely down to the bottom of the pan so you fully cut through the crust.* ABOVE, RIGHT *Remove the finished piece by pressing up through the bottom of the cookie cutter. Note that this technique is perfect for all the tarts and quiches in this book and many of the desserts.*

Mushroom Tart

THERE ARE people who love anything (everything) chocolate. For them, too much chocolate is never enough. For people who love mushrooms, the same applies. This tart is an adaptation of the mushroom duxelles I mentioned earlier that I use to stuff chicken breasts or pipe on top of a bland piece of fish. This tart is easy—good either hot or cold, a welcome addition to a buffet, a first course, or a main course for lunch or dinner. Even that *b(runch)* word comes to mind.

YIELD: *8 to 10 servings*

1 stick (8 tablespoons) salted butter
2 pounds medium fresh mushrooms, minced
1¼ teaspoon salt plus a pinch of salt, divided
½ cup sherry
4 eggs
2 cups heavy cream
1 teaspoon white pepper

1 teaspoon beef stock base (see note, page 4)
2 bunches green onions, the last two inches cut off, the rest chopped to the end of the white part
¼ pound grated Gruyère cheese, firmly packed
Basic Pâte Brisée (page 268)

Preheat the oven to 325°F.

In a large, heavy skillet over a medium heat, melt the butter and, when the foaming has subsided, add the mushrooms and ½ teaspoon of the salt. Turn the heat to medium-low and sauté the mushrooms very slowly, about 20 minutes, until all the liquid has evaporated.

Add the sherry and continue to sauté the mushrooms until all the liquid has evaporated and there is no more steam coming off.

In a medium mixing bowl, whisk together the eggs, cream, ¾ teaspoon of the salt, the white pepper, and the beef stock base.

Stir in the green onions and the cheese, and then the mushrooms.

Pour the mixture into the prebaked 9 × 13-inch pastry shell and bake it for approximately 30 minutes, until it's firm. Let the tart cool for at least 15 minutes, before slicing it into whatever size pieces you desire and serving it warm or cold.

Brooke's "Confetti" Grits

BROOKE HAYWARD has been a close friend for nearly twenty years. Her mother was 1930s mega–movie star Margaret Sullavan, who had, at one time been married to Henry Fonda and William Wyler before she married Brooke's father, the über-agent blockbuster-producer Leland Hayward, who did the stage productions of *The Sound of Music*, *My Fair Lady*, and *Gypsy*, and the film version of *Mister Roberts*. Brooke was married to, among others, *Easy Rider* star Dennis Hopper, and has three wonderful children, Jeffrey, Willie, and Marin, all of whom I consider to be like family to me. Brooke wrote a best-selling book about her unusual life of privilege and pain, *Haywire*, which, if you have a dysfunctional family, and I am not sure who doesn't, I suggest you read. To boot, she is an excellent hostess, and a talented, intuitive cook. Here is an adaptation of her recipe for grits that she often serves to any and all who are lucky enough to know her.

(continued on next page)

Brooke Hayward, at twenty-two, in Long Island, 1959

(continued from previous page)

YIELD: *6 to 8 servings*

4 tablespoons salted butter, plus
more for baking dish

3 cups chicken stock

¾ cup coarse stone-ground yellow
grits or polenta

1 teaspoon salt

1 cup grated Cheddar cheese, firmly
packed

½ cup grated Parmesan cheese,
firmly packed

1 cup crème fraîche

3 eggs, beaten

2 teaspoons minced garlic

¼ teaspoon cayenne pepper

1¾ cups chopped green onions

1 cup chopped red bell pepper

1¼ cups chopped green bell pepper

3 cups corn, blanched and chopped
(about 4 ears)

Preheat the oven to 350°F.

Butter a 13 × 9 × 2-inch baking dish.

In a medium stockpot over high heat, bring the chicken stock to a boil. Turn
the heat down, add the grits, and stir. Cook the grits for 8 to 10 minutes, until
most of the stock is absorbed, but they are still runny.

In a large mixing bowl, combine the salt, Cheddar and Parmesan cheeses,
crème fraîche, beaten eggs, garlic, cayenne pepper, green onions, red and green
peppers, and corn.

Add the grits and fold the ingredients together until they are well combined.

Pour the mixture into the prepared baking dish and bake it for 50 to 60
minutes, until it has set.

Dorothy's Baked Cheese Grits

BY NOW, if you have read any part of this book, you probably know that Dorothy was my mother's amazing cook when I was growing up and an inspiration to me in many ways. Since most of her recipes were never formally written down, I re-created the taste I remembered, and please, Dorothy, when you read this from Heaven, if I messed up, forgive me! I serve these grits with Erlinda's Exquisite Short Ribs (page 239) for a hearty winter dinner, with Roasted Pork Tenderloin with Cilantro Lime Butter (page 254), or frankly with just about anything. It's impossible to go wrong.

YIELD: *6 to 8 servings*

½ cup milk

6 cups chicken stock

1 teaspoon salt

½ teaspoon ground black pepper

⅛ teaspoon cayenne pepper

2 teaspoons minced garlic

2 cups regular grits, not instant

½ pound crumbled blue cheese

½ pound Gruyère cheese, grated

½ pound grated very sharp Cheddar cheese, plus 4 tablespoons

1 tablespoon grated Parmesan cheese, firmly packed

1 stick (8 tablespoons) salted butter, plus more for the casserole dish

2 teaspoons Dijon mustard

1 tablespoon lemon juice

4 large eggs, beaten

Preheat the oven to 350°F. Butter a 2-quart casserole dish.

In a medium pot over a medium heat, bring the milk, chicken stock, salt, black pepper, cayenne pepper, and garlic to a boil.

Add the grits and turn the heat to low. Cover the pot and cook the grits for 6 to 8 minutes, stirring every few minutes so there won't be lumps.

Turn off the heat and let the grits rest for 5 minutes.

Stir in the blue, Gruyère, ½ pound of the Cheddar, and Parmesan cheeses, along with the butter, mustard, and lemon juice. Let the grits cool, about ten minutes, and then stir in the beaten eggs.

Pour the grits into the buttered casserole dish, and top them with 4 tablespoons Cheddar.

Bake the grits for 40 minutes until they are set. Remove them from the oven, let them cool for 25 minutes, and serve.

My Take on
Charleston Shrimp and Grits

IN CHARLESTON, shrimp and grits are often called "breakfast shrimp." Usually it is a stew of tomatoes, red and green peppers, and onions with shrimp over creamy, stone-ground grits. It's delicious but, frankly, it can't hold a candle to the lush, creamy velouté below. I serve this as a wintry lunch dish, and, even though it is probably more appropriate in the daytime, I do not hesitate to serve it as part of a big dinner buffet.

YIELD: *4½ cups, or 6 to 8 servings*

1¾ cups milk

1¾ cups chicken stock

1 cup heavy cream

¼ cup plus 2 tablespoons lemon juice

½ cup plus 2 tablespoons grated
   Parmesan cheese, firmly packed

½ teaspoon minced garlic

½ teaspoon plus ⅛ teaspoon salt

½ teaspoon white pepper

3 tablespoons salted butter

3 tablespoons flour

2½ pounds medium (26 to 30 count)
   shrimp

½ cup basil chiffonade

Grits cooked according to package
   directions, allowing about
   3 ounces per person

In a heavy, medium saucepan over medium heat, warm the milk, chicken stock, cream, lemon juice, Parmesan cheese, garlic, salt, and white pepper, until they are just beginning to scald.

Melt the butter in a small, heavy skillet over medium heat and add the flour to make a roux. Stir with a wooden spoon or rubber spatula until it is fully cooked through but not brown.

Add the roux to the milk mixture, and bring it to a boil.

Turn off the heat and stir in the shrimp. They will cook in the warm liquid without additional heat.

Stir in the basil and serve over the grits.

5

Sauces

I'll admit it: I am a sauce freak. A little sauce can transform the merely good into the extraordinary, or even the bad into the good. Both cases are worth the small amount of extra calories. Please don't be afraid of sauce. It's worth it. Another thing to consider: if you make a sauce well, people may believe that you are actually a better cook than you are, as many cooks shy away from them because they fear sauces are too complicated. In these pages, I have tried to make them easy. Each and every one is beloved, with many general and specific uses. Please note that for lots of these recipes, there are yet again themes and variations; if you maintain the basic proportions so that they hold up, feel free to experiment with ingredients and flavorings. By the end of this chapter, I'd wager and hope that you, too, will be a sauce freak like me!

OPPOSITE *This Perfect Homemade Mayonnaise is the basis for so many sauces.*

Perfect Homemade Mayonnaise

I CAN'T say enough about the difference between homemade and store-bought mayonnaise. With no disrespect to Hellmann's (Best Foods, west of the Rockies), which is an excellent product and one I use often, the difference between the two is something that is truly a game-changer. Once you've had the homemade version, it's very hard to ever go back. It's utterly worth the small effort to make it—and I do mean small, as in less than three minutes. With the aid of your favorite food processor, you will have an incredibly silky, lemony, fresh emulsion that can easily be flavored in endless ways to suit your purposes. Add to that the pride of having mastered it yourself, and I know you'll really love the whole thing!

YIELD: *1 cup*

3 egg yolks
4 tablespoons lemon juice
1¼ teaspoon Dijon mustard
¼ teaspoon dry mustard

¾ teaspoon salt
⅛ teaspoon black pepper
¾ cup tasteless vegetable oil
(see note, page 4)

In the bowl of a food processor fitted with the metal blade, combine the egg yolks, lemon juice, Dijon mustard, dry mustard, salt, and black pepper.

Process these ingredients for approximately 2 minutes, until the yolks are thick and sticky.

Continue to process the yolks, adding the oil slowly in a steady stream, through the feed tube of the processor, making sure that all the oil is incorporated. When all the oil has been added, the mayonnaise should be thick, luxurious, and fully emulsified.

Herb Mayonnaise

To the previous perfect homemade mayonnaise recipe add any or all of the ingredients listed below—there is no wrong way to do this; experiment with what you like the best. Let the result rest overnight, covered, in your refrigerator so that all flavors can steep and you will have a fully realized flavor.

2 tablespoons fresh chopped tarragon	1 tablespoon minced garlic
2 tablespoons fresh basil chiffonade	1 tablespoon minced shallots
2 tablespoons fresh chopped dill	2 tablespoons chopped parsley

NOTE You will probably like a bit more salt after you have added these herbs, shallots, and parsley, but it is really best to let these flavors rest as long as you can. I always try to make herb mayonnaises the day before serving, and generally don't even taste them to correct the seasonings until it's time to serve.

Shallots are an integral part of any herb mayonnaise.

Perfect Hollandaise Sauce
and Variations

AUGUSTE ESCOFFIER (1846–1935), credited with formalizing what we know today as traditional French cuisine, took regional French traditions and standardized their forms. He changed the way a commercial kitchen was run, dividing it into parts with a sous-chef in charge of each part. There was a sauce chef, a sauté chef, a pastry chef, and a *garde-manger*, who oversaw cold plates. His innovations are still in place in most restaurant kitchens today. Hollandaise sauce is merely one of thousands of Escoffier's entries in his seminal masterpiece *Le Guide Culinaire*, which every serious cook should read. Here's my interpretation of what very well may be the best of all classic sauces.

This sauce, sadly, is one that is rare these days. I grew up on it and I truly miss it. In our house, hollandaise sauce made everything better: asparagus, broccoli, poached salmon, even sautéed mushrooms and toast in the morning. This recipe is crazy easy, despite what people say. If you follow these directions, you can do it, just be sure to keep whisking the sauce over low heat so that the butter and eggs become fully emulsified, not scrambled.

YIELD: *1 cup*

4 egg yolks	Pinch ground white pepper
1 tablespoon water	8 tablespoons salted butter
½ teaspoon salt	2 tablespoons lemon juice

Prepare a double boiler over medium heat.

In a medium mixing bowl, combine the egg yolks, water, salt, and pepper. Beat them with a whisk until they are very thick and sticky. This may also be done in an electric stand mixer fitted with the whisk attachment. Pour the eggs into the double boiler and turn the heat down to low.

(continued on page 134)

OPPOSITE *Perfect Hollandaise Sauce starts with gorgeous eggs.*

(continued from previous page 131)

In a heavy skillet, over a high heat, melt the butter. When it is fully melted and bubbling, add it slowly in droplets to the egg yolk mixture, whisking it constantly over very low heat until an emulsion forms. Do not add the butter too quickly, and make sure the heat is not too high, or you will have scrambled eggs instead of hollandaise sauce.

Stir in the lemon juice and serve the sauce immediately, or add the ingredients for the variations—mustard sauce, mousseline sauce, béarnaise sauce, or sauce choron—listed below.

Mustard Sauce

This sauce is perfect for grilled sole, or a cheese soufflé.

To Perfect Hollandaise Sauce, add:

7 tablespoons Dijon mustard
½ teaspoon lemon juice

¼ teaspoon cayenne pepper

Mousseline Sauce

Amazing decadence on a spinach soufflé or a salmon soufflé.

To Perfect Hollandaise Sauce, add:

½ cup cream, whipped stiff

⅛ teaspoon salt

Béarnaise Sauce

The perfect sauce for grilled or roast beef, but I really love it best on simply grilled salmon steaks or fresh Florida grouper.

To Perfect Hollandaise Sauce, add the reduction below. In other words, boil the following ingredients down to about 1 tablespoon, which should take about 15 minutes in a heavy saucepan over high heat:

⅛ teaspoon black pepper
⅛ teaspoon salt
¼ cup white wine
¼ cup white wine vinegar

1 tablespoon minced shallot
1½ teaspoons dried tarragon

OPPOSITE *Sauce Choron, a tomato-flavored Hollandaise sauce, is excellent with any grilled fish or chicken.*

Sauce Choron

To Béarnaise Sauce add:

3 tablespoons tomato paste   ⅛ teaspoon salt
2 teaspoons lemon juice

Perfect Beurre Blanc and Variations

ONE OF the most beloved dishes at The Patio by the River was a "Trio of Grilled Fish" served with an accompanying "trio" of flavored beurre blancs. Beurre blanc is literally "white butter" in French, a pungent sauce made from a reduction of shallots and white wine, which are later emulsified with cold butter. For stability, I add the smallest bit of cream here, as it keeps this temperamental sauce from separating on its reheat. Our "trio" changed every day, but it was usually salmon, grouper, and snapper. The delicious sauces were plain beurre blanc, dill beurre blanc, and red pepper beurre blanc. It didn't matter in the least which sauce went with which fish: they became interchangeable.

YIELD: *10 to 12 servings*

4 shallots, minced
2 cups white wine
½ cup lemon juice
2 tablespoons heavy cream
¾ teaspoon salt

¼ teaspoon ground white pepper
4 sticks (24 tablespoons) salted butter, cold and cut into small cubes

---

In a heavy saucepan over a high heat, combine the shallots, wine, and lemon juice. Reduce the mixture until it is thick and syrupy and measures approximately ¼ cup. This will take about 20 minutes.

Reduce the heat to very low, and add the cream, salt, and pepper. Whisk in the cubed butter, a little at a time.

When the butter is fully combined and the mixture is emulsified, remove it from the heat. Serve the sauce immediately, or store it in a thermos until you are ready to serve.

Variations

To the finished sauce, add ½ cup of any of the following ingredients

Chopped chives
Chopped dill

Basil chiffonade
Pureed roasted red bell peppers

A trio of Beurre Blancs. Left to right: *red pepper, plain, and dill*

Cucumber Sauce

THIS FANTASTIC cold sauce is a perfect dip for crudités, excellent on cold chicken or fish, or even good on Lavash crackers. Make sure to follow the instructions to a T, as too much leakage from the cucumbers will make it bitter, not scrumptious.

YIELD: *4 to 6 servings*

1½ pounds English cucumbers (approximately two cups, peeled and seeded)
1¼ teaspoons salt, divided
2 tablespoons chopped dill
2 tablespoons minced shallots

1 tablespoon lime juice
1 teaspoon lime zest
¾ cup sour cream
¾ cup plain yogurt
¼ cup mayonnaise
⅛ teaspoon ground black pepper

Peel and seed the cucumbers. Sprinkle them with 1 teaspoon of the salt, and let them drain on a rack for at least 45 minutes.

Dice half of the cucumbers by hand and, in a food processor fitted with a metal blade, puree the other half. Drain the diced cucumbers with a cheesecloth.

In a medium-sized mixing bowl, combine the cucumbers with the rest of the ingredients, and let the sauce chill for several hours before serving.

ABOVE, LEFT *Make sure you drain all the excess liquid out of the cucumbers. Here they are before being squeezed through cheesecloth.* ABOVE, RIGHT *See what I mean?!*

Sex is good . . .

but not as good as fresh, sweet corn!

GARRISON KEILLOR

6

Vegetables and Side Dishes

I have never been able to stand vegetable recipes from the South. Vegetables are cooked for hours in salt pork or, even worse, fatback, making them lifeless and limp, fatty and with all of the nutrients boiled out of them. You will not find any recipes for those unmentionables here, but instead, easy guidelines for what I consider to be the perfect ways to serve delectable vegetables and grains as side dishes or first courses. Please note that I have included many different potato recipes, because potatoes are, hands down, my absolute favorite.

OPPOSITE *Heirloom Tomato Pie (page 173) just before it goes in the oven*

143

Gratin Dauphinois,
aka "Potatoes Patio"

IF I had nothing else to eat in my life, I think these potatoes would be enough. Yes, they are rich. Very! And they fall under the category of CSE (Can't Stop Eating . . .). At The Patio by the River, we served them with nearly every main dish, cut into a diamond-shaped wedge. To me, the best part, not unlike with a properly gratinéed onion soup, is the cheese when it gets brown and crusty. . . . I could go on and on, but I am sure you get the picture. They are perfect with just about anything, and are equally good cold, tomorrow, from the refrigerator. There's just no way to go wrong here.

YIELD: *10 to 12 servings*

Butter for the baking dish
2 cups heavy cream
1¾ teaspoons salt
¾ teaspoon black pepper
1½ teaspoons minced garlic
¼ teaspoon ground nutmeg

3 pounds baking potatoes, scrubbed, peeled, and sliced paper thin, lengthwise (see note)
1 pound grated Gruyère cheese
2 tablespoons grated Parmesan cheese

Preheat the oven to 375°F. Butter a 13 × 9 × 2-inch baking dish.

In a medium mixing bowl, whisk together the cream, salt, pepper, garlic, and nutmeg.

Assemble one layer of potatoes on the bottom of the buttered baking dish.

Gently spoon ⅛ cup of the cream mixture over the layer of potatoes. Top with some grated Gruyère.

Repeat this process until the dish is full and the potatoes and cream mixture are exhausted. Top with remaining Gruyère and 2 tablespoons of Parmesan.

Cover the baking dish with aluminum foil and bake it for 1 hour. Remove the foil and continue to bake for another 15 to 20 minutes, until the top is crusty and brown, and serve.

NOTE A mandoline is most helpful for slicing the potatoes.

Marguerite's Twice-Baked Potatoes

MARGUERITE LITTMAN has been called "the Belle of Chester Square." She hails from Monroe, Louisiana, and when she speaks, quite honestly it sounds as if she never left there, although she has spent most of her life in England. After a stint in Hollywood (where, among other things, she coached Elizabeth Taylor, for *Cat on a Hot Tin Roof*, on how to "speak Southern," a technique Marguerite and Tennessee Williams developed as follows: "You *hit* the verbs, slur the nouns, and go up—as an ascending scale would do—at the end of the sentence!"), Marguerite, a stylish, magical character, emerged as the wife of one of the most revered London barristers, confidante to Diana, Princess of Wales, and Elton John alike, and one of London's great hostesses. Let's not forget her philanthropy: She started the AIDS Crisis Trust in England, which has now folded into The Elton John AIDS Foundation. With the help of Victor and Carmen, Marguerite serves the most delicious, simple, chic, and often Southern food, and is renowned in discriminating circles for her wit, charm, kindness, wisdom, and a term she taught me, her "zigzag."

YIELD: *6 to 8 servings*

2½ pounds russet potatoes
½ cup milk
6 tablespoons salted butter, melted
2 tablespoons plus 1½ teaspoons
    sour cream
3 tablespoons chopped chives
3 tablespoons grated Parmesan
    cheese, firmly packed

1 teaspoon salt, plus more for
    the skins
½ teaspoon ground black pepper,
    plus more for the skins
¼ cup grated Cheddar cheese,
    firmly packed

Preheat the oven to 350°F.

On a baking sheet, bake the potatoes for 1½ hours, until they are soft to the touch. Remove them from the oven and let them cool.

When they are cool, cut them in half lengthwise and scoop out the insides of the potatoes, leaving about ¼ inch of potato on the skin. Place the scooped potato in a medium mixing bowl.

To the scooped-out potatoes, add the milk, melted butter, sour cream,

(continued on next page)

(continued from previous page)

chives, Parmesan, 1 teaspoon salt, and ½ teaspoon black pepper. Mash the potatoes with a potato masher.

Season the potato skins with salt and pepper to taste, and then refill the skins with the mashed potatoes. If you feel creative, use a pastry bag. Garnish the potatoes with the grated Cheddar and bake at 350°F for 10 minutes.

Turn the oven to broil and place the potatoes on the highest rack of the oven. Broil them until they are golden brown, 3 to 5 minutes, and serve.

Louisiana belle Marguerite Littman with Princess Diana, London, 1996

Nan's Baked Potatoes with Caviar

I'VE ALREADY told you what a fantastic hostess Nan Kempner was, and I have included several recipes that she inspired in this book. People often said of her, to paraphrase Rudyard Kipling, "though she walked with kings, she never lost the common touch." I absolutely loved it when, at Christmas time, for lunch, Nan would serve these baked potatoes with caviar. It was the way that they were served that was such fun. First you would get a plain baked potato. Next, huge tins of Russian or, in those days, Iranian caviar would be passed as many as five or six times so gluttons like me could take as much as we liked. Then more. Nan had an intuitive understanding of quality and luxury, and she wore it lightly, and always with an irreverent sense of humor.

YIELD: *6 servings*

6 russet potatoes

The best and the most expensive caviar your budget allows

Crème fraîche

Snipped chives for garnish

Bake the potatoes, cut them open, and serve them with the caviar, crème fraîche, and chives.

After a fun dinner: Nan Kempner at home in New York with me (left) and Peter Bacanovic (right), June 2000

My Hash Brown Cake

FANCY STEAK-HOUSE style, these are the full extent of my fried potatoes. I don't make French fries or homemade chips, because lots of other people do them much better. These, however, I'll put up against anyone's. The secret to these is twofold: hot clarified butter and pressing the potatoes down in the pan so that they sear to form a crusty exterior, and then weighing them down so that they steam on the inside (see note). Serve them with anything, even eggs, but I always like them best with beef and lamb.

YIELD: *One large cake, 6 to 8 servings*

2 pounds russet potatoes
2 tablespoons salted butter
¾ cup diced yellow or white onions
1½ teaspoons salt
¾ teaspoon ground black pepper

2 tablespoons grated Parmesan cheese, firmly packed
5 tablespoons clarified butter, available at most upscale grocery stores

Bring a large pot of water to a boil. Peel the potatoes.

Steam the peeled potatoes over the boiling water for 14 minutes exactly.

In a medium skillet over medium high heat, melt the butter. When the foaming has subsided, add the onions and sauté them until they are translucent, 3 to 5 minutes.

Grate the steamed potatoes using a grater or a food processor.

In a large mixing bowl, combine the sautéed onions, salt, pepper, grated potatoes, and Parmesan cheese. Toss them to mix them together well.

In a heavy skillet over high heat, heat the clarified butter. When the pan is hot, press the potato mixture firmly into the pan. Turn the heat down to medium.

Cook the potatoes over medium heat until they are brown and crusty, approximately 10 to 15 minutes. Lift the potato cake from the pan and, before you flip it, add the remaining clarified butter to the pan. Flip the potato cake and cook until the other side is brown. Remove it from the pan and let it rest for at least 5 minutes before cutting it into whatever size pieces you desire.

NOTE I find these potatoes are much better if you weigh them down while you are cooking them. Do this with a heavy skillet or a cake pan or anything else that will apply pressure to the potatoes. Also, I call for medium heat but medium-low may work better, as the potatoes will get crustier on the outside.

Mashed Potatoes with Maytag Blue

THESE ARE nothing short of awesome. Maytag Blue is made at the May-tag Dairy Farms in Newton, Iowa, and is a superb cheese that I would put up for the blue ribbon against any of its foreign colleagues: Gorgonzola, Stilton, or Roquefort. This cheese actually started as an experiment by one of the members of the Maytag appliance family who had heard about an innovative cheese-making process circa 1941, and it is still made by hand in small batches in virtually the same fashion today. I often send it to friends at Christmas. My mother served these potatoes with beef tenderloin (page 235) and they always disappeared. They are very easy, and are better, like so many things in this book, when done ahead of time.

YIELD: *4½ cups, or about 8 servings*

4 cups water

2½ teaspoons salt, divided

3 pounds baking potatoes

6 tablespoons salted butter,
  plus more for the baking dish

¼ cup milk

¼ cup cream

¼ teaspoon ground white pepper

5 ounces crumbled Maytag blue
  cheese

1 tablespoon grated Parmesan
  cheese, firmly packed

Coarsely ground black pepper

In a medium stockpot over high heat, bring 4 cups water and 1½ teaspoons of the salt to a boil.

Peel the potatoes and cut them into large chunks. Reduce the heat to medium and add the potatoes to the boiling water.

Simmer them until they are very tender and easily pierced by a fork. They should have no resistance left. This should take between 10 and 20 minutes.

Remove the potatoes from the heat, drain them in a colander, and put them in a large mixing bowl.

Add 4 tablespoons of the butter, the milk, cream, ½ teaspoon of the salt, and the white pepper to the hot potatoes. Mash them with a potato masher until they are smooth.

Preheat the oven to 300°F. Butter an 8-cup baking dish, spoon in half of the mashed potatoes, and top with 2 ounces of crumbled Maytag blue cheese.

Spoon the remaining mashed potatoes on top of the cheese. Top with the remaining 3 ounces of Maytag blue, the Parmesan, the remaining 2 tablespoons of butter, and lots of coarsely ground black pepper. I find this pepper, combined with the Maytag blue cheese and Parmesan, is what makes this dish soar, so don't be shy with the pepper grinder.

Bake the potatoes for 15 to 20 minutes, until the cheese has started to melt and is golden brown, and serve.

You can't ever go wrong with meat and potatoes. I love these Mashed Potatoes with Maytag Blue with Perfect Roast Tenderloin of Beef (page 235), pictured here with Orange Mayonnaise (page 128).

Caroline's Soubise

THIS IS my mother's recipe, and the aroma of its cooking can send me quickly back to childhood. I remember thinking it was so sophisticated— little did I know that this dish couldn't be easier. It's a household dish in France, and one that far too few Americans know. A masterpiece of braised rice and onions, it's risotto's first cousin, though infinitely easier, and, unlike risotto, possible to do ahead. I am even going to go out on a limb and say it's not only better when done the day before, but even two days before. It's one of my most treasured dishes, and I hope it will give you and your family as much happiness as it has mine.

Whenever I smell this dish cooking, I am three years old again.

4 quarts water

1½ tablespoons plus 3 teaspoons salt, divided

¾ teaspoon ground black pepper

1 cup rice (see note)

1 stick (8 tablespoons) salted butter

14 cups sliced onions

1¼ teaspoons ground black pepper

½ cup grated Gruyère cheese, firmly packed

Preheat the oven to 300°F.

In a large stockpot over high heat, bring 4 quarts water and 1½ tablespoons of the salt to a boil. Drop the rice into the rapidly boiling water and boil it for 5 minutes exactly. Drain the rice immediately in a colander and reserve.

In a large Dutch oven over medium-high heat, melt the butter. When the foaming has subsided, add the onions, 1 teaspoon of the salt, and ½ teaspoon of the black pepper. Turn off the heat and toss the onions in the butter to coat them thoroughly.

Add the parcooked rice and cover the Dutch oven tightly. Put it in the preheated oven and bake it for 1½ hours. Remove it from the oven and let the rice cool—I suggest overnight.

When it's time to serve, add the grated Gruyère, the remaining teaspoon of salt, ¾ of the remaining teaspoon of black pepper, reheat it, and serve it warm.

NOTE I usually use jasmine, but Carolina long grain or any white rice (as long as it's not instant) would be good in this recipe.

Sour Cream Corn Cakes

THESE EXTRAORDINARILY light pancakes are so simple to make, and perfect with pork, smoked salmon, or, my favorite, crème fraîche and salmon roe. Make these ahead and then reheat them slightly, add a generous dollop of crème fraîche and a heaping helping of salmon caviar and some chopped chives on top, and you'll have one of the easiest, most impressive first courses known to man. Let me know when you're serving it—I'll really want to come for dinner!

YIELD: *12 cakes*

1 quart water
1 tablespoon salt
1 cup corn
1 cup sour cream
1 egg, beaten
2 tablespoons melted salted butter

1 teaspoon baking powder
1 teaspoon baking soda
1½ teaspoons salt
⅛ teaspoon ground black pepper
¼ cup chopped green onions
½ cup all-purpose flour

In a medium stockpot over a high heat, bring 1 quart water and the salt to a boil. Drop the corn into the water and boil it for 2 minutes exactly. Drain the corn in a colander, and dry it thoroughly.

In a medium-sized mixing bowl, whisk together the sour cream, egg, melted butter, baking powder, baking soda, salt, and pepper. Stir in the corn and the green onions.

Through a sieve, shake the flour over the mixture, and stir until it is just combined. Do not overmix or the cakes will be chewy and tough. Yuck!

Over a medium heat, heat a heavy nonstick skillet. Pour in 3 tablespoons batter for each cake, and cook them about 2 minutes per side, until they are golden brown. Serve either warm or cold.

Silver Queen Corn Pudding

THIS DISH goes with everything. I love it with plain grilled fish, in the height of the summer corn season, accompanied by the juiciest summer tomatoes. Silver Queen is my favorite of all corn, so that's the one I cite, but this formula will work for any corn, even frozen—but please don't say I said so.

YIELD: *6 to 8 servings*

Butter for the baking dish
1 quart water
1 tablespoon salt plus 1½ teaspoons, divided
3 cups corn, such as Silver Queen, fresh yellow summer corn, or good-quality frozen
1½ cups heavy cream
1½ cups milk

3 tablespoons salted butter, melted
1½ tablespoons sugar
⅜ teaspoon ground black pepper
5 eggs, beaten
3 tablespoons minced onion squeezed dry in cheesecloth, and measured afterwards
1½ teaspoons flour

Preheat the oven to 300°F. Butter an 8-cup soufflé dish or two 4-cup soufflé dishes.

Bring 1 quart water and 1 tablespoon of the salt to a boil in a medium stockpot over high heat.

Drop in the corn and blanch it for 2½ minutes exactly, then drain it in a colander, making sure you get out all the excess water.

Puree the corn in a food processor fitted with a metal blade until the kernels are no longer whole, but not yet smooth. Drain the puree thoroughly in a colander.

In a large mixing bowl, combine the corn, cream, milk, melted butter, sugar, salt, black pepper, eggs, and minced onion, and the remaining 1½ teaspoons of salt, and stir. Shake the flour over the mixture and stir it gently in to combine.

Pour the mixture into the prepared baking dish and bake it for about 45 minutes, until the custard is just set. It should still tremble a small bit. Serve.

OPPOSITE *After you cut the corn from the cob, make sure to scrape down the sides with your knife to get all the excess corn milk.*

Pumpkin Pecan Flan with Roquefort

GROWING UP in the South, we never had pumpkin anything. It wasn't until I spent my first Thanksgiving in New York, and then in Los Angeles, that I had pumpkin in the fall with any regularity. Here's a recipe I devised several Thanksgivings ago to punch up the flavor of regulation canned pumpkin with the warmth of my favorite nut, the pecan, and the tang of delectably indescribable French Roquefort.

YIELD: *6 to 8 servings*

1 (15-ounce) can pure pumpkin
3 large eggs
2 egg yolks
½ cup heavy cream
2 tablespoons minced fresh ginger
½ teaspoon salt
¼ teaspoon ground black pepper
1 tablespoon plus 1 teaspoon sugar

½ cup crumbled Roquefort
   (or other blue cheese)
¼ cup roasted pecans
2 tablespoons chopped chives
   for garnish
Crème fraîche or sour cream
   for garnish

Preheat the oven to 350°F. Butter an 8-cup soufflé dish or two 4-cup soufflé dishes.

Combine the pumpkin, eggs, yolks, heavy cream, ginger, salt, black pepper, and sugar in a food processor fitted with a metal blade and process until smooth.

Pour the mixture into the prepared baking dishes and assemble a bain-marie (see note below).

Top the pumpkin mixture evenly with the crumbled Roquefort and then the roasted pecans.

Bake for 35 to 40 minutes, until barely still trembling; bake for 5 to 10 minutes, less time if you will reheat it the next day.

Serve warm, garnished with the chives and crème fraîche.

ASSEMBLING A BAIN-MARIE Note: it sounds fancy, but it's very easy, and makes such a difference in cooking perfect custards, that you owe it to yourself to learn how. Place a soufflé dish into a deep roasting pan, and pour boiling water into the sides of the pan, so the water comes about a quarter of the way up the sides of the soufflé dish. Be very careful when you put the bain-marie in the oven so you don't burn yourself!

Heirloom Tomato Pie

LATE SUMMER is the height of tomato season, and I love to make this pie using any variety and color of tomatoes. I cite heirlooms here, as they are automatically varied in size and color, and provide a natural gorgeousness without your having to scrounge your greengrocer's aisles for assorted tomato varieties. Feel free, however, to experiment with any variety you like. Sometimes I add sliced cherry or pear tomatoes or, if I am lucky enough, home-grown tomatoes from the garden of a friend more disposed and able to grow such things than I am!

YIELD: *8 to 10 servings*

2 pounds mixed heirloom tomatoes

1½ teaspoon salt, divided

2 tablespoons salted butter

1 onion, halved, then sliced thin

2 teaspoons minced garlic

1 cup Perfect Homemade Mayonnaise (page 126)

1 cup fresh basil leaves, firmly packed

3 sprigs fresh parsley

1 medium shallot, peeled

1 green onion, whole

1 cup grated Gruyère cheese, firmly packed

1 cup grated sharp Cheddar cheese, firmly packed

½ cup plus 1 tablespoon grated Parmesan cheese, divided

Basic Pâte Brisée (page 268)

1 to 1½ tablespoons coarsely ground black pepper

Slice the tomatoes into ¼-inch-thick slices and place them on a rack to drain. Sprinkle the tomatoes on both sides with ¾ teaspoon salt, 1½ teaspoons total. Let them drain on the rack for at least an hour to remove the unwanted water.

When the tomatoes have finished draining, preheat the oven to 375°F. In a heavy skillet over medium-high heat, melt the butter. When the foaming has subsided, add the onions and sauté them for a couple of minutes, until they are slightly soft, and then add the minced garlic. Continue to sauté the onions and garlic until they are translucent, 10 to 12 minutes.

In the bowl of a food processor fitted with a metal blade, combine the mayonnaise, basil leaves, parsley, shallot, and green onion, and process them until the mixture is green and smooth, approximately 1 minute.

(continued on next page)

(continued from previous page)

ABOVE, LEFT *Cut the tomatoes into ¼-inch-thick slices.* ABOVE, RIGHT *On a cooled, prebaked pastry shell, spread the mayonnaise and cheese mixture . . .*
OPPOSITE, TOP LEFT *. . . and then add the sautéed garlic and onions on top.*
OPPOSITE, TOP RIGHT *Arrange the sliced tomatoes on top of the sautéed garlic and onions.* OPPOSITE, BOTTOM LEFT *Coarsely grind fresh pepper on top of the tomatoes.*
OPPOSITE, BOTTOM RIGHT *And then sprinkle with 1 tablespoon Parmesan cheese before baking.*

In a large mixing bowl, combine the mayonnaise mixture with the Gruyère, Cheddar, and ½ cup of the Parmesan cheese and stir to mix thoroughly.

Spread the cheese mixture evenly over the cooled pastry crust.

Place the sautéed onions and garlic evenly on top of the cheese mixture, and then arrange the drained tomatoes in a pretty pattern on top.

Sprinkle with the remaining 1 tablespoon Parmesan cheese and the black pepper, and bake the pie for 50 to 60 minutes.

Let the heirloom tomato pie rest for at least 30 minutes before cutting, and serve it warm, at room temperature, or cold with additional basil mayonnaise, some of which you will have left over if you made your own!

Magnificent Broccoli Puree

SOMETIMES, THE simplest recipes become magnificent. This recipe is one of those. It goes with everything, in all seasons.

YIELD: *6 to 8 servings*

2 quarts water
1 tablespoon plus 1 teaspoon salt

2½ pounds broccoli
¼ cup heavy cream

In a large pot over a high heat, bring 2 quarts water and 1 tablespoon of the salt to a boil.

Drop the broccoli into the boiling water, and boil it for about 5 minutes, until it is tender.

Remove it from the heat and drain in a colander.

In a food processor fitted with a metal blade, puree the broccoli in batches until it is smooth. Transfer it to a medium mixing bowl, add the cream and the remaining teaspoon salt, stir it well, and serve. You can also let it cool, reheat it, and serve it later.

Carrot Puree with Ginger

HOW TO make a simple carrot puree soar? Add ginger. I have flavored this dish with lots of fresh ginger, which makes it different and really good, so please know that if you like ginger, you'll absolutely love it. I serve this all year long and, more often than not, with the broccoli puree, and you can see how gorgeous they look together. One of my very favorite menus is these two dishes with Chicken Chasseur (page 214).

YIELD: *6 to 8 servings*

2 quarts water
1 tablespoon plus ½ teaspoon salt
2 pounds carrots

2 tablespoons salted butter
2 tablespoons minced fresh ginger

In a large pot over high heat, bring 2 quarts water and 1 tablespoon of the salt to a boil.

Peel the carrots and then chop them into large chunks. Drop them into the boiling water and boil them until they are tender, approximately 12 to 13 minutes. Remove them from the heat and drain them in a colander.

In a food processor fitted with a metal blade, combine the carrots, butter, the remaining ½ teaspoon salt, and the ginger, and puree until smooth.

Serve immediately, or let the carrots cool and reheat them when it's time to serve.

FOLLOWING SPREAD *Carrot Puree with Ginger and Magnificent Broccoli Puree are excellent together—and gorgeous!*

Stewed Tomatoes

THIS IS an integral part of my Southern Menu, one that I often serve for large buffets. I often combine stewed tomatoes with Dorothy's Fried Chicken (page 203), Pulled Pork with Carolina Barbecue Sauce (page 250), My Take on Charleston Shrimp and Grits (page 122), Silver Queen Corn Pudding (page 166), Broccoli Slaw (page 66), and Herb Biscuits (page 261). Let's note that the lore of many Southern cooks dictates that, nutritionally, if you get your colors "right," you've gotten your dinner "right," so these tomatoes are just the right addition to all those delectables above.

YIELD: *6 to 8 servings*

4 tablespoons salted butter, plus more for the baking dish
2 (28-ounce) cans whole tomatoes, or whole plum tomatoes, thoroughly drained
1 tablespoon minced shallots
1 teaspoon dried tarragon
2 tablespoons brown sugar
1¾ teaspoons salt
½ teaspoon freshly ground black pepper

Preheat the oven to 350°F. Butter a 13 × 9 × 2-inch baking dish.

Assemble the tomatoes, shallots, and tarragon in the bottom of the prepared baking dish. Add the sugar, salt, and pepper and toss them thoroughly so that the tomato mixture is fully coated.

Cut the butter into small pieces and spread it over the top.

Place the dish in the preheated oven and bake it for 1½ hours, until the top is somewhat caramelized from the brown sugar. Serve.

Penne with Vodka Sauce

THIS IS another favorite recipe from Connie Wald, the ultimate Hollywood hostess (see Connie's Chocolate Sauce, page 324). She often serves this as a first course, and when she doesn't, people always wonder where it is. Even Nancy Reagan takes seconds. I like lots of cracked black pepper and extra Parmesan on top, and have a very hard time keeping my portions small and polite.

YIELD: *about 16 servings*

1 pound dried penne pasta

1 stick (8 tablespoons) salted butter

2 cups diced onions

1 cup vodka

2 (28-ounce) cans crushed tomatoes

2 tablespoons double-strength
   tomato paste

2 teaspoons red pepper flakes

1½ teaspoons salt

2 cups heavy cream

1 cup shredded Parmesan cheese

Cook the penne al dente, according to the package directions. Make sure the water is salted: rule of thumb, 1 tablespoon of salt for each quart of water. Reserve the cooked penne.

In a large skillet over medium heat, melt the butter. When the foaming has subsided, add the onions and sauté them until they are slightly brown and soft, approximately 10 to 12 minutes. Add the vodka and continue to sauté another 10 minutes, until the onions are very soft.

Add the tomatoes, tomato paste, red pepper flakes, and salt, and let the mixture simmer for about 30 minutes, until it has reduced by about a third. Add the heavy cream and let the sauce simmer for another 30 minutes.

Remove the sauce from the heat, stir in the Parmesan cheese, and serve it over the cooked penne.

In the hands of an able cook, fish can become

an inexhaustible source of perpetual delight.

BRILLAT-SAVARIN

7

Seafood

I am old enough to remember the days when seafood seemed much more exotic than it does now. Salmon was a delicacy, and shrimp, crabmeat, and lobster seemed like luxuries. In brasseries and bistros in France, salmon was always served with béarnaise sauce (page 134), and that's how I fell in love with it. I can eat béarnaise sauce on just about anything. If halibut had come that way, there is no question I would have liked it better than I do.

In the South when I was growing up, most seafood restaurants were fry houses at beaches, every greasy menu item accompanied by hush puppies and coleslaw. Not so at The Patio by the River—our Pecan-Crusted Salmon (page 195) was made with wild Norwegian salmon, the freshest Georgia pecans, minced garlic, and dill. It's a standout, but so are all the recipes in this chapter. They're exactly what I love: ideas that are steeped in tradition yet contemporary in their flavorings.

Creamed Shrimp with Country Ham

THIS DELICACY says "spring lunch" to me. I have a memory of it from a limpid late spring day many years ago in a beautiful plantation house in Newnan, Georgia, about an hour south of Atlanta. There was lovely Empire furniture, an exquisite table, family silver, and huge double damask linen napkins. And then came the lunch: the inspiration for this recipe was served over rice with spinach and biscuits, and I thought it was such a simple, flavorful, evocative dish that I reimagined it here for this book. The original version didn't have dill or tomato paste, but I think you'll be pleased with those additions. This dish would make a very nice first course at dinner, and could even be served over grits or polenta as yet another version of the ever-popular shrimp and grits.

YIELD: *6 to 8 servings*

6 tablespoons salted butter

1 cup diced onion

2 pounds medium (26 to 30 count) shrimp, peeled and cleaned

¼ cup dry sherry

1½ teaspoons salt

¾ teaspoon ground black pepper

¾ cup heavy cream

4 tablespoons tomato paste

3 tablespoons chopped fresh dill

¼ pound country ham, diced

In a heavy skillet over medium heat, melt the butter. When the foaming has subsided, add the onions. Sauté them until they are translucent, about 10 minutes.

Add the shrimp, sherry, salt, and pepper, and sauté them until the shrimp are just slightly pink, about 4 minutes.

Add the heavy cream and tomato paste, and continue to sauté for another 2 to 3 minutes, until everything is well combined.

Remove the skillet from the heat and stir in the dill and country ham.

Serve over rice.

Crabmeat Mornay

MORNAY, A béchamel sauce with the addition of cheese, is a very traditional, delicious French treat, perhaps named for a sixteenth-century Duc de Mornay, a powerful potentate, perhaps named for a pair of nineteenth-century dandies and brothers, the Marquis de Mornay and the Comte de Mornay. It doesn't matter how it was named: this dish is sufficiently rich, stylish, and delicious that either strain of the Mornay family would be delighted to take credit for it.

YIELD: *8 to 10 servings*

1½ cups heavy cream, divided
2½ cups milk, divided
16 tablespoons salted butter, divided
¾ cup flour
1¼ teaspoons salt
⅜ teaspoon cayenne pepper
1 tablespoon dried tarragon

1¼ cups grated Gruyère cheese, firmly packed
2 pounds jumbo lump crabmeat, thoroughly picked over
½ cup brandy
5 egg yolks

Preheat the oven to broil. In a medium stockpot over medium heat, combine 1 cup of the cream with 2 cups of the milk until they are just scalding.

Melt 8 tablespoons of the butter in a medium skillet over medium heat, and add the flour to make a roux. Stir it with a wooden spoon or a rubber spatula until it is fully cooked through but not brown. This will take 3 to 4 minutes.

Add the roux to the scalding milk and cream, and whisk it thoroughly to get the lumps out. Then add the salt, cayenne pepper, and tarragon.

Bring the mixture to a boil and then remove it from the heat and let it cool slightly before stirring in the Gruyère cheese. In a large, heavy skillet over medium heat, melt the remaining 8 tablespoons of the butter. When the foaming has subsided, add the crabmeat and brandy. Sauté for approximately 2 minutes, until the crabmeat is thoroughly bathed in the butter and the brandy.

In a medium mixing bowl, combine the egg yolks with the remaining ½ cup cream and ½ cup milk, and then add it to the cheese mixture.

Pour the crabmeat with the butter and the brandy into a 13 × 9 × 2-inch baking dish, pour the sauce over the crabmeat, and blend it gently so as not to break up the lumps. Broil for 5 to 8 minutes, until the top is brown in places and bubbly, and serve.

Lobster Thermidor

ORIGINALLY CREATED in 1894 in a Paris restaurant across the "Place" from the Comédie-Française on the same night that a play called *Thermidor* opened, the traditional version is lobster meat with a Mornay sauce, brandy, egg yolks, mustard, and cheese on top. Mine differs from the original in several ways. I have added mushrooms, tarragon, and lemon juice, and removed the egg yolks, and I am confident that you will never miss them. Broil this dish to make it brown on top and serve it to your guests as a luxurious first course for dinner or a wintry main dish indulgence at lunch.

YIELD: *8 to 10 servings*

2 cups milk

1 cup heavy cream

14 tablespoons salted butter, divided

¾ cup flour

¼ teaspoon cayenne pepper

¼ teaspoon nutmeg

1 tablespoon dried tarragon

¾ teaspoon dry mustard

1½ teaspoons Dijon mustard

3 teaspoons salt, divided

2 teaspoons lemon juice

1½ cups grated Gruyère cheese, firmly packed

1½ pounds mushrooms, halved

¾ teaspoon ground black pepper

2 pounds lobster meat

6 tablespoons brandy

Preheat the oven to broil.

In a medium stockpot over medium heat, heat the milk and cream until they are just scalding.

Melt 8 tablespoons of the butter in a medium skillet over medium heat, and add the flour to make a roux. Stir it with a wooden spoon or a rubber spatula until it is fully cooked through. This will take 3 to 4 minutes.

Add the cayenne pepper, nutmeg, tarragon, dry mustard, Dijon mustard, and 1½ teaspoons of the salt.

When the roux is fully cooked through and a pale golden brown, add it to the milk-cream mixture, whisking it vigorously to break up the lumps, and then bring it to a boil.

Immediately remove the pot from the heat and let it cool slightly, and then stir in the lemon juice and the Gruyère cheese.

In a medium skillet over medium-high heat, melt 3 tablespoons of the butter. When the foaming has subsided, add the mushrooms, ½ teaspoon of the salt, and ¼ teaspoon of the black pepper. Sauté until all the liquid has been released from the mushrooms, about 5 minutes. Drain the mushrooms in a colander and then add them to the sauce.

In another heavy skillet over medium heat, melt the remaining 3 tablespoons butter. When the foaming has subsided, add the lobster, the remaining 1 teaspoon salt, the remaining ½ teaspoon black pepper, and the brandy. Sauté the lobster for about 3 minutes, until it is fully bathed in the butter and brandy, but be careful when you stir it because the meat can break easily.

Pour the lobster into a 13 × 9 × 2-inch baking dish, and then pour the sauce over the top, stirring gently to combine.

Broil it for 5 minutes, until portions of the top are bubbling and brown, and serve immediately.

Dover Sole Florentine

I HAVE always wondered why dishes that add spinach are characterized as "Florentine." My best guess is that it has to do with Catherine de Medici (1519–1589), the Florentine wife of French king Henry II (1519–1559), who brought spinach with her when she came to France from Italy. Keep the Creamed Spinach with Artichokes in the freezer for when you have that lovely piece of fresh sole, or any other fish or chicken, for that matter, that you don't quite know how to handle.

YIELD: *6 to 8 servings*

2 pounds Dover sole, cut into 4- to
    5-ounce fillets
1 teaspoon salt

½ teaspoon ground black pepper
½ recipe Creamed Spinach with
    Artichokes (page 170)

Preheat the oven to 450°F.

Butter a 13 × 9 × 2-inch ceramic baking dish. Season both sides of the fish with the salt and pepper and then place the seasoned filets in the prepared baking dish. Spread 2 to 3 ounces creamed spinach with artichokes evenly over each fillet.

Bake the sole for 8 to 10 minutes, and then serve it immediately.

Sautéed Chilean Sea Bass
with Beurre Blanc

I OFTEN serve this in the summer when it's hot and I can get the freshest Chilean sea bass. Always remember that fish should be treated with respect, never overcooked, and eaten when it is ready. This fish is moist and flavorful, and this preparation makes it even more so. For me, the tanginess of the beurre blanc is the ideal accompaniment.

YIELD: *6 to 8 servings*

4 tablespoons clarified butter
3 tablespoons flour
2 teaspoons salt
1 teaspoon ground black pepper
2 pounds Chilean sea bass, cut into
    4- to 5-ounce fillets

Perfect Beurre Blanc (page 136)
Chopped chives or chopped parsley
    for garnish

In a large, heavy skillet over medium-high heat, heat the clarified butter. In a shallow dish, whisk together the flour, salt, and pepper.

Dredge the sea bass fillets through the flour mixture on both sides, shaking to remove the excess flour.

When the butter is hot, just before it bubbles, add the sea bass fillets and sauté them for 3 to 4 minutes per side, until they are golden brown but still thoroughly moist on the inside.

Remove the fillets from the pan, place them on a warm serving platter, top them with the beurre blanc, garnish with chopped chives or parsley, and serve.

Pecan-Crusted Salmon
with Sauce Gribiche

IF WE were speaking in theatrical terms, this dish would be referred to as a "set piece." That's the piece of business that comes in the middle of an act that is the standout, the thing to which all moments lead up to, and descend from. This fish is that piece of business.

The garlic, dill, and pecans are in amazing harmony together. You won't go wrong with this salmon without sauce gribiche, but once you put the sauce gribiche on, Katie, bar the door! Sometimes disparate elements combine into magic, and that is exactly what has happened here. I discovered this winning combination quite by accident, in the process of testing both recipes on the same day for this book. Who knew they would be such a winning combination? There's no way to go wrong either way, but do yourself a favor and serve them together.

YIELD: ¾ cup (exactly enough for one 2-pound
salmon fillet to serve 8 to 10 people)

PECAN TOPPING
¾ cup whole pecans
1 teaspoon minced garlic
¾ teaspoon salt
¾ teaspoon dried dill
3 tablespoons salted butter, melted

SALMON
1 (2-pound) boneless skinless salmon
   fillet
½ teaspoon salt
¼ teaspoon ground black pepper
1 recipe Sauce Gribiche (page 129)

Preheat the oven to 400°F.

Combine the pecans, garlic, salt, dill, and melted butter in the bowl of a food processor fitted with a metal blade and process them until they resemble coarse crumbs.

Season the salmon on both sides with the salt and black pepper. Spread the pecan mixture evenly on top of the seasoned salmon fillet and place the salmon on a large baking sheet. Bake it for 10 to 11 minutes, until it is cooked through but still rare, and then serve it hot with sauce gribiche.

OPPOSITE *Pecan-Crusted Salmon with Sauce Gribiche*

Salmon Pot Pie

EARLY ON in developing products for The Beverly Hills Kitchen, I invented this dish. I wanted an updated pot pie and this one is full-flavored and delicate yet hearty and a departure from the traditional idea. A helpful note here is that, just like the Chicken Pot Pie (page 205), this dish can be done ahead and then frozen for whenever you need it. I tend to serve it in the colder months, usually with a simple green salad or Perfect Asparagus (page 171).

YIELD: *One 13 × 9 × 2-inch pie, 8 to 10 servings*

MASTER LIST OF INGREDIENTS

1½ cups chicken stock
1 cup heavy cream, divided
½ cup plus 2 tablespoons white
    wine, divided
1 tablespoon dried dill
2⅛ teaspoons salt, divided
½ pound frozen pearl onions
6 tablespoons salted butter, divided
2 tablespoons minced shallots
¾ pound mushrooms, cut in half

6 tablespoons flour
1½ tablespoons vermouth
¼ cup lemon juice
1 cup half-and-half
1⅛ teaspoons ground black pepper
2 pounds fresh salmon, cut into
    2-inch chunks
¾ pound grape tomatoes
3 tablespoons freshly chopped
    parsley

Preheat the oven to 425°F.

1½ cups chicken stock
½ cup heavy cream
½ cup white wine

1 tablespoon dried dill
1 teaspoon salt

In a medium pot over medium-high heat, bring the above ingredients to a boil.

To the boiling liquid, add

½ pound frozen pearl onions

and blanch them for 2 minutes exactly. Drain the onions in a colander and reserve the liquid. In a large skillet over medium-high heat, melt

(continued on page 198)

(continued from page 196)

2 tablespoons salted butter

and when the foaming has subsided, add the pearl onions. Sauté for 2 minutes exactly, and then add

2 tablespoons minced shallots	½ teaspoon salt
¾ pound mushrooms, cut in half	

and sauté these ingredients for another 2 minutes exactly. Then turn off the heat.

In a medium skillet over medium-high heat, melt

4 tablespoons salted butter	6 tablespoons flour

until you have a roux that is thoroughly cooked through and pale golden brown. Then add

2 tablespoons white wine	1 cup half-and-half
1½ tablespoons vermouth	⅛ teaspoon salt
¼ cup lemon juice	1⅛ teaspoons ground black pepper
½ cup heavy cream	

In a medium stockpot over medium-high heat, combine all the reserved liquid from above, the sautéed mushrooms and onions, and the roux, and bring the mixture to a boil until the sauce has just thickened.

Turn the heat off, and then add

2 pounds fresh salmon, cut into 2-inch chunks	¾ pound grape tomatoes
½ teaspoon salt	3 tablespoons chopped parsley

Stir them together until they are well combined. Do not overstir or the salmon will become shredded. Pour the salmon stew into a 13 × 9 × 2-inch baking dish, top with the biscuit crust and egg wash (recipe follows), and bake it for 20 to 25 minutes, until brown and bubbling.

Biscuit Crust for Salmon Pot Pie

2 cups all-purpose flour
½ teaspoon sugar
1¼ teaspoons salt
1 tablespoon plus ⅛ teaspoon baking
    powder (make sure it's new!)
1 stick (8 tablespoons) salted butter,
    cold and cut into quarters

¾ cup cold milk
2 tablespoons chopped parsley
2 tablespoons chopped chives

Egg wash: 1 beaten egg plus
    1 tablespoon heavy cream

In the bowl of a food processor fitted with a metal blade, combine the flour, sugar, salt, and baking powder, and pulse them a couple of times, until they are fully combined.

Add the cold butter, all at once, and pulse until it resembles coarse crumbs, about 8 to 10 times.

Pour the milk through the feed tube slowly, while pulsing. This will take approximately 20 to 25 pulses. Pea-size crumbs will form. Do not continue pulsing until the dough pulls away from the sides of the bowl, or the biscuits will be tough.

Pour the pea-size crumbs onto a floured surface, and then add the parsley and chives.

Gather the crumbs together, kneading the dough 2 to 3 times, maximum. Do not overknead the dough, or the biscuits will be tough.

Roll the dough out to ¼- to ½-inch thickness, and place it over the salmon stew.

Brush the top generously with the egg wash, and bake it for 20 to 25 minutes, until it's brown and bubbling.

Dorothy's Fried Chicken

THIS FRIED chicken was part of the menu Dorothy left for us, as I mentioned with the Squash Casserole recipe (page 165), on her days off.

I have re-created what I believe to be her fried chicken, punched up with onions and garlic, which she certainly did not use, and without buttermilk, which she certainly did. If you have all night to soak the chicken in buttermilk beforehand, go for it. I don't. I don't have nearly enough patience or forethought. This is superlative chicken—a buttermilk brining may or may not make it better. In other words, don't bother unless you want to, but feel free to try.

YIELD: *One 4- to 5-pound chicken, cut into 8 pieces.*
How many that serves is up to you . . .

1 fryer chicken (4 to 5 pounds), cut into 8 pieces, gizzard discarded
1½ teaspoons plus 2 tablespoons salt, divided
½ teaspoon plus ⅓ cup ground black pepper, divided
1 cup minced onion
½ cup minced garlic

4 cups all-purpose flour
2 tablespoons dried oregano
2 tablespoons paprika
1 tablespoon chili powder
2 to 3 quarts vegetable oil for frying
4 eggs
3 cups milk

Rinse the chicken and pat it dry thoroughly.

In a large mixing bowl, combine the chicken, 1½ teaspoons of the salt, and ½ teaspoon of the black pepper, the onions, and the garlic. Toss these ingredients together thoroughly.

In a container big enough to hold all the chicken pieces (a bowl, preferably with a top, or a Rubbermaid container with a top, or a bowl that can be covered with plastic wrap or aluminum foil), whisk together the flour, the remaining 2 tablespoons salt, the remaining ⅓ cup black pepper, the dried oregano, paprika, and chili powder.

In a very heavy, large pot or a deep skillet over medium-high heat, bring the oil to 325°F exactly, using an instant-read candy thermometer (a meat thermometer will not measure a high enough temperature).

While the oil is heating, in a small mixing bowl, whisk together the eggs

(continued on next page)

(continued from previous page)

and milk. Pour them over the chicken, and let it soak for at least 20 minutes.

Remove the chicken from the egg mixture and place it in the container in which you have mixed the dry ingredients.

Cover the container and shake the chicken until it is fully coated.

Remove the chicken pieces from the bowl and place them again in the egg mixture, tossing delicately to coat them, but not so much as to remove the coating.

Put the chicken back into the dry mixture, cover it, and shake it again. By now there should be a thick coating on the chicken. Add the chicken to the oil, in batches, and fry it until it is light brown, more than golden, and the internal temperature is at least 155°F per piece. This will take approximately 8 to 10 minutes for thighs, a little less for drumsticks and wings, and perhaps up to 15 minutes for breasts. It is very important to maintain the oil temperature at around 325°F so that the chicken will not burn.

Drain it on a rack, let it rest for at least 15 minutes, and then serve.

ABOVE, LEFT *Make sure you use a candy thermometer to measure the temperature of the oil because a meat thermometer does not go up high enough.* ABOVE, RIGHT *Always use tongs because the oil is really hot.*

Chicken Pot Pie

CHICKEN POT PIE may be the ultimate comfort food. Nancy Reagan served this dish (her version, not mine) at many California governor's mansion and White House dinners. When I entertained her for the first time at home, I considered showing off with something a bit more high-toned, but I quickly thought better of it. If it's good enough for Mrs. Reagan, it's good enough for me. This is my twist on the American classic, Frenched-up and Southerned-up. There are many steps, but none are particularly hard. Follow each step carefully, and the result will be perfect.

YIELD: *One 13 × 9 × 2-inch pie, 8 to 12 servings*

MASTER LIST OF INGREDIENTS

3¼ cups chicken stock

¾ cup white wine

1½ tablespoons plus ½ teaspoon dried tarragon, divided

2½ teaspoons salt, divided

1 pound boneless, skinless chicken breasts

1⅝ teaspoons ground black pepper, divided

2 medium carrots (approximately ¾ pound), sliced on the diagonal or diced

½ pound frozen pearl onions

6 tablespoons salted butter, divided

¾ pound sliced mushrooms

½ cup flour

1 cup heavy cream

4½ tablespoons golden sherry

4½ tablespoons lemon juice

½ teaspoon nutmeg

1½ tablespoons snipped chives

3 tablespoons chopped parsley

10 ounces frozen baby peas

Egg wash: 1 beaten egg plus 1 tablespoon heavy cream

Preheat the oven to 450°F.

3 cups chicken stock

¾ cup white wine

1½ tablespoons dried tarragon

1½ teaspoons salt

In a medium stockpot over high heat, bring the chicken stock, wine, tarragon, and salt to a boil. Add

(continued on next page)

(continued from previous page)

1 pound boneless, skinless chicken
    breasts

and slowly simmer, just below full boil, for 4 minutes exactly. Remove them from the liquid, turn down the heat to low, and reserve the chicken.

Let the chicken rest for at least 5 minutes, and then either shred it or cut it into 1½-inch chunks. It will still be raw on the inside.

Place the chicken in a medium mixing bowl and add

¼ teaspoon salt   ⅛ teaspoon ground black pepper

and toss well. Back to the stove: turn the heat up to medium-high, and add

2 medium carrots (about   ½ pound frozen pearl onions
    ¾ pound), sliced on the
    diagonal or diced

and blanch them for 2 minutes exactly. Drain them in a colander and reserve the carrots, onions, and the liquid. In a large skillet over medium heat, melt

2 tablespoons salted butter

and when the foaming has subsided, add the carrots and onions and sauté for another 2 minutes exactly. Then add

¾ pound sliced mushrooms   ¾ teaspoon salt

and sauté the vegetables for another 2 minutes. Turn off the heat and reserve. In a medium skillet over medium-high heat, melt together

½ stick (4 tablespoons) salted   ½ cup flour
    butter

to make a fully-cooked-through, pale-golden-brown roux. Pour the reserved liquid into a medium stockpot and bring it to a boil over medium-high heat. Add the roux to the boiling liquid, whisking vigorously to break up the lumps, and then add

1 cup heavy cream   ½ teaspoon nutmeg
4½ tablespoons golden sherry   1½ teaspoons ground black pepper
4½ tablespoons lemon juice   ½ teaspoon dried tarragon

and bring it to a boil until it has just thickened. Add all the vegetables and the chicken, and let the mixture simmer over medium heat for about 5 minutes, until the chicken is fully cooked through. Remove the pot from the heat and let it cool for at least 15 minutes, and then stir in

1½ tablespoons snipped chives   3 tablespoons chopped parsley

When the mixture is fully cool, another 15 to 20 minutes or so, stir in

10 ounces frozen baby peas

and then pour the mixture into a 13 × 9 × 2-inch baking dish. Roll out the biscuit dough (recipe follows), place it on top, and brush it with the

Egg wash: 1 beaten egg plus
    1 tablespoon heavy cream

Bake for 20 to 25 minutes, until it is golden brown and bubbling. Let it rest for at least 5 minutes, and then serve.

Biscuit Crust for Chicken Pot Pies
(do ahead of making the chicken stew)

2 cups all-purpose flour
½ teaspoon sugar
1¼ teaspoons salt
1 tablespoon plus ⅛ teaspoon baking
    powder (make sure it's new!)

1 stick (8 tablespoons) salted butter,
    cold and cut into quarters
¾ cup cold milk
2 tablespoons chopped parsley
2 tablespoons chopped chives

In the bowl of a food processor fitted with a metal blade, place flour, sugar, salt, and baking powder, and pulse a couple of times, until they are fully combined.

Add the cold butter, all at once, and pulse until it resembles coarse crumbs, 8 to 10 times.

Pour the milk into the top sleeve, slowly, while pulsing, until the milk is completely added. This will take 20 to 25 pulses. Pea-size crumbs will form. Do not continue pulsing until the dough pulls away from the sides of the bowl, or the crust will be tough.

Pour the pea-size crumbs onto a floured surface, and then add the parsley and chives.

Gather the crumbs together, kneading the dough 2 or 3 times, maximum. Do not overknead the dough, or the crust will be tough.

Chicken Shiitake Chili

THIS EASY recipe is a new take on chili. The mushrooms give this earthy dish a reassuring body and underlying flavor that make it irresistible. It freezes spectacularly, and with a green salad and some crostini, it is a perfect dinner or lunch in the winter when it's cold, yet it is light enough for the warmer months.

YIELD: *12 cups, or 12 to 16 servings*

MASTER LIST OF INGREDIENTS

2 pounds boneless, skinless chicken breasts

3⅞ teaspoons salt, divided

⅝ teaspoon ground black pepper, divided

½ stick (4 tablespoons) salted butter, divided

4 cups diced onions

2 tablespoons minced garlic

1 pound shiitake mushrooms, sliced

2 red bell peppers, diced

2 yellow bell peppers, diced

1 teaspoon chili powder

1⅛ teaspoons cumin, divided

2 28-ounce cans whole tomatoes, undrained

1 cup chicken stock

¼ teaspoon cayenne pepper

1 teaspoon lemon juice

3 tablespoons balsamic vinegar

2 tablespoons dark brown sugar

½ teaspoon dried thyme

---

2 pounds boneless, skinless chicken breasts

1¼ teaspoons salt, divided

½ teaspoon plus ⅛ teaspoon ground black pepper, divided

½ stick (4 tablespoons) salted butter, divided

4 cups diced onions

2 tablespoons minced garlic

1 pound shiitake mushrooms, sliced

2 red bell peppers, diced

2 yellow bell peppers, diced

1 teaspoon chili powder

1 teaspoon cumin

2 28-ounce cans whole tomatoes, undrained

1 cup chicken stock

¼ teaspoon cayenne pepper

Season each side of the chicken with ⅛ teaspoon of the salt and 1/16 teaspoon of the black pepper, for a total of ¼ teaspoon salt and ⅛ teaspoon black pepper.

Melt 2 tablespoons of the butter in a large, heavy skillet over medium-high heat. When the foaming has subsided, add the chicken to the skillet and sear it for approximately 3 minutes per side, until it is crusty and brown on the outside but still raw on the inside. Remove from the heat, let it rest for at least 10 minutes, and reserve.

In a large, heavy stockpot over medium-high heat, melt the remaining 2 tablespoons of the butter. When the foaming has subsided, add the onions and sauté for approximately 5 to 6 minutes, until they are soft. Add the garlic, mushrooms, red peppers, and yellow peppers, and sauté for 4 to 5 minutes, until the onions become translucent. Then add the chili powder, cumin, tomatoes, chicken stock, the remaining 1 teaspoon salt, and the remaining ½ teaspoon black pepper, and the cayenne pepper. Shred or dice the chicken, whichever you prefer, and add it to the pot. Let this simmer for about 40 minutes over medium to medium-low heat. Then add

2½ teaspoons plus ⅛ teaspoon salt	3 tablespoons balsamic vinegar
1 teaspoon lemon juice	2 tablespoons dark brown sugar
⅛ teaspoon cumin	½ teaspoon dried thyme

and bring the mixture to a boil again. Let it cool and store it covered in the refrigerator overnight. Reheat the chili and serve it tomorrow or the next day. The longer you wait, the better the flavor will be.

Texas Ranch Chicken

THIS SUMPTUOUS dish is a staple in Texas circles and has made its way into the collective food consciousness of America because, frankly, it was just too good to stay down on the farm! The lore is that this dish first appeared on the tables at the King Ranch, one of the largest cattle ranches in the world, some 825,000 acres, and was so popular that it was copied by everyone who had been lucky enough to sample it while visiting. It spread and spread and, by the 1950s, it had degenerated into something whose "secret" ingredient was a can of Campbell's Cream of Mushroom soup. Let's rewind. I loved the idea of it and went back and rejiggered it. This is a do-ahead, freezable dish for all ages. It's decadent, and, like Texas itself, full of big, strong characters!

YIELD: *10 to 12 servings*

6 tablespoons salted butter
3 garlic cloves, minced
2¼ teaspoons chili powder
6 tablespoons flour
2 cups very rich chicken stock
½ cup white wine
1¾ teaspoons salt, divided
1 teaspoon ground black pepper, divided
½ cup sour cream
3 tablespoons extra-virgin olive oil
1 green bell pepper, diced
1 medium onion, diced
1 cup thickly sliced mushrooms
2 pounds cooked, seasoned chicken breasts, shredded or diced
2 (10-ounce) cans RO*TEL tomatoes and green chiles, drained
3 tablespoons sherry
1¾ teaspoons cumin
1 teaspoon lemon juice
4 tablespoons chopped cilantro
1 cup chopped green onions

8 ounces sharp Monterey Jack cheese, shredded, divided
8 ounces sharp Cheddar cheese, shredded, divided

10 soft corn tortillas, cut into eighths

In a heavy medium stockpot over medium heat, melt the butter. When the foaming has subsided, add the garlic and chili powder, and sauté for 3 to 4 minutes, until the garlic becomes fragrant.

Add the flour, stirring thoroughly. Then immediately add the chicken stock, white wine, ½ teaspoon of the salt, ¼ teaspoon of the black pepper, and the sour cream, and bring to a boil. Turn off the heat and reserve.

In a large skillet over medium heat, heat the olive oil, and just before it begins to bubble, add the bell pepper, onion, and mushrooms. Sauté them until they are soft, approximately 6 to 8 minutes.

Add the chicken, tomatoes, the remaining 1¼ teaspoons salt, the remaining ¾ teaspoon black pepper, sherry, cumin, and lemon juice. Continue to sauté these ingredients for 3 to 4 minutes, until everything has combined well. Turn off the heat and then stir in the cilantro and green onions.

In a large mixing bowl, combine the vegetables and the sauce and stir well.

Preheat the oven to 350°F. In a small mixing bowl, combine the jack and Cheddar cheese together.

In a 13 × 9 × 2-inch baking dish, arrange a layer of tortillas, then a layer of the chicken mixture, and then a layer of cheese. Repeat this process, topping the mixture with a final layer of cheese.

Bake the casserole until it is golden brown and bubbling, about 20 to 25 minutes, and then serve it hot.

I love to serve simple food on a formally set table. Here it's Chicken Pot Pie with a green salad and David Jones's fantastic flowers.

Chicken Hash

THERE ARE two inspirations for my chicken hash, the '21' Club and the Carlyle Hotel, both in New York City. I feel lucky to have enjoyed both many times, and confident enough in this recipe that, at the Posh Restaurant Dish Regatta, I am convinced this boat would take "first." The Carlyle serves theirs with foie gras on top, truly a luxury, and an embodiment of the high-low juxtaposition I find so appealing in food. I prefer it with steamed or sautéed spinach and brown rice as a main dish for lunch or dinner.

YIELD: *8½ cups, or 10 to 12 servings*

10 tablespoons salted butter, divided
½ pound mushrooms, quartered
2 tablespoons minced shallots
½ cup sherry
2½ cups milk
1½ cups heavy cream
2½ teaspoons salt
¼ teaspoon ground black pepper
¼ teaspoon cayenne pepper
¼ cup plus 2 tablespoons flour

3 tablespoons Parmesan cheese, divided
1¼ cups grated Gruyère cheese, firmly packed
1 cup grated Gruyère cheese, firmly packed, divided
2 pounds cooked chicken (page 7), shredded
4 tablespoons chopped fresh basil
1 tablespoon chopped parsley

Preheat the oven to 375°F.

Melt 2 tablespoons of the butter in a large skillet over medium heat. When the foaming has subsided, sauté the mushrooms and the shallots for 5 to 7 minutes, until they are soft. Add the sherry and sauté for another 2 minutes. Turn off the heat and reserve.

Combine the milk, heavy cream, salt, ground black pepper, and cayenne pepper in a medium stockpot over medium heat.

Melt the remaining 8 tablespoons butter in a medium skillet over medium heat, and add the flour to make a roux. When it is fully cooked through and pale golden brown, add the roux to the milk mixture, whisking vigorously to break up the lumps, and bring it to a boil. The sauce will have thickened. Let it cool for about 3 minutes, and then stir in 2 tablespoons of the Parmesan and ¾ cup of the Gruyère cheese.

Combine the mushrooms and shallots with the shredded chicken in a large mixing bowl. Pour the cheese sauce over the chicken and stir well to combine.

Pour the entire mixture into a deep 13 × 9 × 2-inch baking dish, and top with the remaining ½ cup Gruyère and 1 tablespoon Parmesan. Bake the hash for 30 minutes, until it is bubbling and brown, and serve it over brown rice with wilted spinach.

Fresh basil is the key to making this chicken hash really special.

Chicken Chasseur

CHASSEUR, LITERALLY "hunter" in French, is a method of preparation that traditionally is made with mushrooms, tomatoes, white wine, and shallots. It says autumn to me, but truly, I think that rule can easily be bent. One of the short cuts I employ as a deviation from the traditional Cuisine Française standard is the addition of beef stock instead of a veal demi-glace for flavor in the sauce. As such, this preparation is extremely easy, yet it tastes as if you have been simmering and prepping for days.

YIELD: *6 servings*

2 tablespoons salted butter
1 tablespoon vegetable oil
2 pounds boneless, skinless chicken breasts (about 3 breasts)
½ teaspoon salt, divided
¼ teaspoon plus ⅛ teaspoon ground black pepper
¼ cup minced shallots
1 teaspoon minced garlic

½ pound sliced mushrooms
¾ pounds firm tomatoes, peeled, seeded, and chopped
¼ cup heavy cream
½ cup white wine
½ cup beef stock
2 tablespoons lemon juice
1 tablespoon flour
2 tablespoons chopped fresh basil

In a large skillet over medium-high heat, melt the butter with the oil. Season the chicken on both sides with ⅛ teaspoon salt and 1/16 teaspoon ground black pepper per side, for a total of ¼ teaspoon salt and ⅛ teaspoon ground black pepper. When the foaming has subsided, sear the chicken on both sides, approximately 3 minutes per side, until a brown crust starts to form.

Remove the chicken from the pan, and add the shallots and the garlic and sauté for 2 minutes. Add the mushrooms and the tomatoes and sauté for about 5 minutes, until they are slightly soft.

Return the chicken to the pan and immediately add the cream, wine, beef stock, lemon juice, the remaining ¼ teaspoon salt, and the remaining ¼ teaspoon black pepper, and continue to sauté for about 6 more minutes, until the chicken is fully cooked but still very moist.

Transfer the chicken to a warm serving platter. Add the flour to the pan to thicken the sauce. Whisk it, and then stir in the basil and spoon the sauce over the chicken. Serve it immediately.

Chicken Country Captain

COUNTRY CAPTAIN is the ultimate in upscale Plantation Cuisine, Charleston style, an onion, bell pepper, curry dish, flavored with currants or raisins. In the South, this dish is "company food," a "better" dish reserved to impress guests when it's time to entertain. It originated in the early nineteenth century in India, as a staple menu item for British colonials. "Country Captain" then came to America as a by-product of the spice trade, and landed in Charleston before spreading throughout the South as standard issue in the art of elegant entertaining. In researching this childhood favorite of mine, I noticed that even the first *Joy of Cooking* featured a bland formula for it. Normally, this fragrant and brilliantly colored stew is served over rice, but to make things easier here, I just went ahead and added the rice to the stew. Please note that this recipe yields lots and lots, but it freezes beautifully and is great to have on hand, "just in case," for those unexpected guests.

YIELD: *12 to 16 servings*

1 pound bulk pork sausage, mild
3 pounds boneless, skinless chicken breasts
2 pounds boneless, skinless chicken thighs
2 teaspoons plus 1 tablespoon salt, divided
2 teaspoons ground black pepper, divided
1½ sticks (12 tablespoons) salted butter, divided
3 cups medium-diced white or yellow onions
1 cup medium-diced red bell pepper
1 cup medium-diced celery
2 tablespoons minced garlic
1½ tablespoons dark brown sugar

1 tablespoon curry powder
1½ teaspoons dried thyme
¾ teaspoon ground cumin
2 teaspoons minced fresh ginger
¾ cup flour
2½ cups tomatoes, peeled (I use good-quality canned ones)
5½ cups chicken stock
2½ cups white wine
½ cup lemon juice
1 tablespoon apple cider vinegar
2 cups golden raisins
4 cups cooked rice
¾ cup snipped chives
1½ cups toasted slivered almonds
½ cup chopped parsley

(continued on next page)

(continued from previous page)

In a large, heavy skillet over medium-high heat, brown the sausage, fully breaking it up, and then drain off the excess fat. Reserve.

Wash the chicken breasts and thighs and pat them dry. Place them in a mixing bowl and toss with 2 teaspoons of the salt and 1 teaspoon of the black pepper.

In another large, heavy skillet over medium heat, melt 4 tablespoons of the butter. When the foaming has subsided, add the chicken and sear it in batches on both sides until it is brown on the surface but still raw inside, about 3 minutes per side. Remove it from the heat, let rest for at least 5 minutes, and then cut it into approximately 1½-inch chunks, and reserve it in a bowl. Do not worry that the chicken is still raw on the inside, as it will finish cooking later.

In a large, heavy stockpot over medium heat, melt the remaining 8 tablespoons butter. When the foaming has subsided, add the onions and sauté for 3 minutes, until they start to get soft. Then add the peppers and celery, and sauté for another 3 minutes. Add the garlic, the remaining tablespoon salt, the remaining teaspoon pepper, the dark brown sugar, the curry, thyme, cumin, and ginger and continue to sauté these ingredients until the onions are translucent, approximately 4 to 8 more minutes. Add the cooked sausage, and then the flour and stir the mixture thoroughly. It will become very thick.

Add the tomatoes, chicken stock, wine, lemon juice, vinegar, and raisins and bring the mixture to a boil. Reduce the heat to a simmer, and continue to simmer the mixture for 5 more minutes.

Add the chicken and simmer the Chicken Country Captain for 5 more minutes, until the chicken is completely cooked through, and then turn off the heat. Stir in the cooked rice, chives, almonds, and parsley, and serve it with buttered crusty French bread.

Chicken Curry

I LOVE chicken curry. There are many variations, but this one is easy, delicious, and may be my very favorite one. I have served it many times for large groups, and there is never any left over. Double this recipe and freeze what you don't use!

YIELD: *6 cups, or 6 to 8 servings*

2 tablespoons salted butter
2 cups medium-diced onions
½ cup diced celery
1 garlic clove, minced
1 tablespoon minced fresh ginger
1 teaspoon curry powder
2 tablespoons tomato paste
¼ teaspoon ground coriander
½ teaspoon cinnamon
¾ teaspoon salt
⅛ teaspoon ground black pepper
⅛ teaspoon cayenne pepper
⅛ teaspoon paprika

1 tablespoon plus ¼ teaspoon flour
2 cups very rich chicken stock
1 tablespoon lemon juice
¼ cup white wine
½ bay leaf
1½ pounds Partially Cooked Chicken breasts (page 7), diced or shredded
1 pound Partially Cooked Chicken thighs (page 7), diced or shredded
½ cup fresh coconut milk
¼ cup chopped cilantro

In a medium stockpot over medium heat, melt the butter. When the foaming has subsided, add the onions and sauté for a couple of minutes, until they have softened a bit. Add the celery and garlic, and continue to sauté until the onions are translucent, approximately 8 to 10 minutes more.

Add the ginger, curry powder, tomato paste, coriander, cinnamon, salt, black pepper, cayenne pepper, and paprika. Stir thoroughly and let them cook for about 1 minute, until well combined.

Add the flour, all at once, and stir. Cook for another minute or so, until it becomes very stiff.

Add the chicken stock, lemon juice, white wine, and bay leaf, turn the heat to medium-high, and let the mixture reduce for 30 to 40 minutes, until it becomes thick and syrupy.

Add the partially cooked chicken breasts and thighs, reduce the heat to medium, and simmer until the chicken is cooked all the way through, 4 to 5 minutes. Turn off the heat and stir in the coconut milk. Serve the chicken curry over rice, garnished with the cilantro.

Parmesan-Crusted Chicken with Lemon Butter

THIS PREPARATION is a cousin of the traditional *francese,* an egg-dipped, battered, sautéed breast finished with a lemon butter pan sauce; its other cousin is piccata. All in the family! I have added Parmesan cheese to the crust here, along with garlic and chopped chives, and am happy to say that this easy preparation is just as much at home on a chicken breast as it is on a veal cutlet. In other words, when you master this treatment for chicken, you automatically have another one up your sleeve for veal . . .

YIELD: *6 to 8 servings*

2 pounds boneless, skinless chicken breasts

2⅛ teaspoons plus 1½ teaspoons salt, divided

1⅛ teaspoons plus ¾ teaspoon ground black pepper, divided

4 eggs

1 cup milk

¾ cup lemon juice, divided

2 tablespoons minced garlic

1 cup grated Parmesan cheese, firmly packed

½ cup all-purpose flour

6 tablespoons salted butter

3 tablespoons olive oil

Chopped chives for garnish

Wash and thoroughly pat the chicken dry.

Butterfly or pound the breasts so they are ¼- to ½-inch thick, and then season both sides with ⅛ teaspoon of the salt and a pinch of the ground black pepper, for a total of ¼ teaspoon salt and ⅛ teaspoon pepper.

In a medium mixing bowl, whisk together the eggs, milk, ½ cup of the lemon juice, garlic, 1¼ teaspoons of the salt, and ½ teaspoon of the black pepper. Set the bowl aside.

In another mixing bowl, whisk together the Parmesan cheese, flour, the remaining 2⅛ teaspoons of the salt, and the remaining 1⅛ teaspoons of the black pepper. Set this bowl aside too.

Melt the butter with the oil in a large, heavy skillet over medium heat.

Dip the chicken in the dry ingredients, coating it on both sides, then in the wet ingredients, then again in the dry ingredients. A thick coating will be evident on the breasts. When the foaming has subsided, sauté the chicken in batches, 3 to 4 minutes per side, until both sides are golden brown.

Transfer the finished pieces to a warm serving platter.

When you are finished sautéing the chicken, deglaze the pan with the remaining ¼ cup lemon juice. Swirl the mixture together, and pour the lemon butter sauce over the top of the breasts. Garnish with the chopped chives, and serve.

Robert's Favorite Turkey Hash

DOROTHY HAD to find dishes that pleased my stepfather, Robert Shaw, whose food tastes were greatly enhanced by my mother's sophistication. Left to his own devices, he might have had nothing but simply prepared steaks or chops with rice or potatoes. Though he loved simpler food, he also learned to appreciate a symphony of great flavors and the integrity of excellent preparation. This dish straddles the line, and was never just reserved for post-Thanksgiving time when there was leftover turkey. He often requested this hash for the post-performance suppers that he had around midnight. This dish can be made days ahead, frozen, and then heated up quickly in a skillet or microwave, and is so flavorful and good that the "everything but the kitchen sink" mundane nature of most hashes is elevated to one that reaches a lemon, thyme, sage, pepper, Parmesan crescendo, one worthy of the palate that has just conducted the Hallelujah Chorus or Mahler's Eighth, the "Symphony of a Thousand."

YIELD: *6 to 8 servings*

MASTER LIST OF INGREDIENTS

3 cups chicken stock

¾ cup white wine

1½ tablespoons dried thyme

2½ teaspoons salt, divided

2 pounds boneless, skinless turkey breast

1⅛ teaspoons ground black pepper, divided

¾ pound frozen pearl onions

5 tablespoons salted butter, divided

6 tablespoons diced red bell peppers

6 tablespoons diced yellow bell peppers

¾ pound sliced mushrooms

6 tablespoons flour

3 tablespoons golden sherry

3 tablespoons lemon juice

½ teaspoon nutmeg

¾ teaspoon ground sage

¾ cup grated Parmesan cheese, firmly packed

1½ tablespoons snipped chives

3 tablespoons chopped parsley

(continued on next page)

(continued from previous page)

3 cups chicken stock	1½ tablespoons dried thyme
¾ cup white wine	1½ teaspoons salt

Bring the chicken stock, wine, thyme, and salt to a boil in a medium stockpot. Add

2 pounds boneless, skinless turkey
    breast

and slowly simmer, just below full boil, for exactly 4 minutes. Remove the turkey from the liquid, keeping the liquid still simmering in the pot, and reserve.

Let the turkey rest for 5 minutes, and then either shred it or cut it into 1½-inch chunks. Place the turkey in a medium mixing bowl, and add

¼ teaspoon salt	⅛ teaspoon ground black pepper

and toss.

To the liquid still boiling in the pot add

¾ pound frozen pearl onions

and blanch them for 2 minutes exactly. Drain them in a colander and reserve both the onions and the liquid. Return the liquid to the stockpot over medium-high heat.

In a large, heavy skillet over medium heat, melt

2 tablespoons salted butter

When the foaming has subsided, add the onions and sauté them for 2 minutes exactly. Then add

6 tablespoons diced red bell peppers	¾ pound sliced mushrooms
6 tablespoons diced yellow bell peppers	¾ teaspoon salt

and sauté for another 8 to 10 minutes, until all the vegetables are soft. Turn off the heat and reserve.

In a small skillet over medium heat, melt together

3 tablespoons salted butter
6 tablespoons flour

until you have a thoroughly cooked, pale golden brown roux. Add the roux to the simmering liquid, whisking vigorously to break up the lumps, and bring it to a boil. Then add

3 tablespoons golden sherry

3 tablespoons lemon juice

½ teaspoon nutmeg

¾ teaspoon ground sage

1½ teaspoons ground black pepper

¾ cup grated Parmesan cheese, firmly packed

and stir well to combine. Add all the vegetables and the turkey, and simmer over medium heat for about 5 minutes, until the turkey is fully cooked through. Remove it from the heat, let it cool for 7 minutes, and stir in

1½ tablespoons snipped chives

3 tablespoons chopped parsley

Serve over brown or white rice.

The short guy on the far left is me, with my stepfather, Robert, President and Mrs. Carter, and members of the Atlanta Symphony Orchestra at the White House following President Carter's inauguration, January 1977

Roulade of Pheasant Breast Stuffed with Spinach and Mushroom Duxelles

THIS DISH comes straight from the pages of The Patio by the River's autumn menu, when pheasant is in season, and it is one of my favorite dishes of all time. Though there are several steps, none is very difficult, and the elegant, full flavors of the stuffing play beautifully against the succulence of the pheasant and the earthiness of the mushroom sauce. A confession: if you are not able to procure pheasant, chicken breasts will work just as well, although I think you will appreciate the subtle differences and will probably not want to ever make this dish differently once you try the pheasant.

YIELD: *10 servings*

10 pheasant breasts, pounded thin
1½ teaspoons salt
½ teaspoon ground black pepper
20 ounces Spinach and Mushroom
    Duxelles (recipe follows)

3 tablespoons salted butter
3 tablespoons vegetable oil

Preheat the oven to 350°F.

Season both sides of the pounded breasts with the salt and pepper, equally.

Spread 4 tablespoons of the spinach and mushroom duxelles in the middle of each breast, and then roll the breasts.

Melt the butter with the oil in a large, heavy skillet. When the foaming has subsided, add the pheasant breasts, and sear them until they are golden brown on both sides, 2 to 3 minutes per side.

Place the breasts on a baking sheet and bake them for 10 minutes.

Remove them from the oven, let them rest for 1 minute, and then slice on the diagonal.

Serve them with Mushroom Sauce (page 231).

Spinach and Mushroom Duxelles

YIELD: *2¾ cups (enough for the previous recipe plus a little extra)*

MASTER LIST OF INGREDIENTS

6 tablespoons salted butter, divided

¾ pound medium mushrooms, minced

1 tablespoon sherry

¾ teaspoon salt, divided

1½ teaspoons minced garlic

1 pound spinach

¾ cup bread crumbs

1 slice crisp bacon, chopped very fine

¼ cup chicken stock, plus
   1½ teaspoons

½ teaspoon sherry

2 tablespoons Parmesan cheese

3 tablespoons chopped green onions

2 tablespoons chopped fresh tarragon

⅛ teaspoon chicken stock base

2 eggs, beaten

⅛ teaspoon ground white pepper

⅛ teaspoon nutmeg

---

3 tablespoons salted butter

¾ pound medium mushrooms, minced

1 tablespoon sherry

¼ teaspoon salt

Melt the butter in a heavy skillet over medium heat. When the foaming has subsided, add the mushrooms and sherry. Turn the heat to medium-low and cook until all of the liquid has been released from the mushrooms and evaporated. This should take 20 to 25 minutes. It's important to get all the liquid out so that the mixture will not be runny.

Turn off the heat, reserve the mushrooms, and let them cool.

3 tablespoons salted butter

1½ teaspoons minced garlic

1 pound spinach

¼ teaspoon salt

Melt the butter in a large Dutch oven over medium heat. When the foaming has subsided, add the garlic, spinach, and salt, and sauté until the spinach is limp, 5 to 7 minutes. Drain the spinach in a colander and reserve it.

(continued on page 230)

FOLLOWING SPREAD *Roulade of Pheasant Breast Stuffed with Spinach and Mushroom Duxelles, with Mushroom Sauce, is perfect for fall and winter.*

(continued from page 227)

When the spinach has cooled, squeeze the excess liquid out by hand so that no liquid remains. Again, this step is very important because you don't want to have a runny stuffing. In a food processor fitted with a metal blade, puree the spinach.

¾ cup bread crumbs

1 slice crisp bacon, chopped very fine

¼ cup plus 1½ teaspoons chicken stock

½ teaspoon sherry

2 tablespoons Parmesan cheese

3 tablespoons chopped green onions

2 tablespoons chopped fresh tarragon

⅛ teaspoon chicken stock base

¼ teaspoon salt

2 eggs, beaten

⅛ teaspoon ground white pepper

⅛ teaspoon nutmeg

In a large mixing bowl, combine the mushrooms, pureed spinach, and all other ingredients.

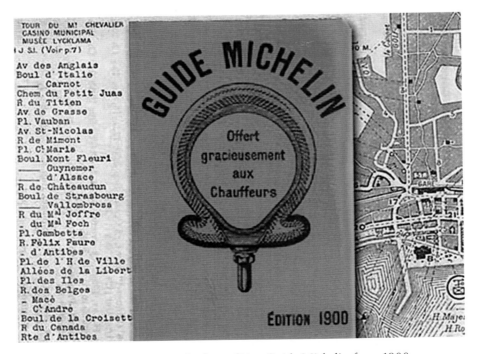

My mother gave me this copy of a first-edition Guide Michelin *from 1900.*

Mushroom Sauce

ONE OF the great food combinations, a magic complement, if you will, is mushrooms with tarragon and cream. This sauce is a staple in France, and one I have loved ever since I first had it when I was traveling with my parents and we stopped at L'Oasis, a Michelin three-star restaurant on the Riviera in a town called La Napoule. It was served over a local sea bass but I love it with pheasant, chicken, or beef just as much.

YIELD: *12 servings, about 4 cups*

5 tablespoons salted butter, divided

3 tablespoons minced shallots

1½ pounds medium fresh mushrooms, divided, half of them minced, the other half of them quartered

1 tablespoon dried tarragon

½ cup plus ½ teaspoon medium dry sherry, divided

2¼ cups rich chicken stock

3 cups heavy cream

¾ teaspoon plus ⅛ teaspoon salt, divided

1¼ teaspoons organic chicken base

½ teaspoon lemon juice

¼ teaspoon ground white pepper

In a large skillet over a medium heat, melt 3 tablespoons of butter and, when the foaming has subsided, add the shallots and sauté them until they are translucent, approximately 2 to 3 minutes.

Add the minced mushrooms, tarragon, and ½ cup of the sherry to the shallots, and cook this mixture slowly until all liquid has evaporated, approximately 30 minutes. Add the chicken stock and increase the heat to high, bringing it to a boil. Let it boil for 10 minutes and then reduce the heat to a simmer and stir in the heavy cream, ¾ teaspoon of the salt, the chicken base, lemon juice, ½ teaspoon of sherry, and white pepper.

Turn off the heat. In a heavy medium skillet over medium heat, melt the remaining 2 tablespoons of butter and, when the foaming subsides, add the ¾ pounds quartered mushrooms and sauté them until they are brown. Add ⅛ teaspoon salt to the mushrooms, stir well, and then add them to the sauce.

Let the sauce cool, cover it, and let it refrigerate overnight. Reheat it and serve.

The only time to eat diet food

is while you're waiting for the steak to cook!

JULIA CHILD

9

Beef, Veal, Lamb, and Pork

I eat chicken and fish more often, but when it's time for beef, nothing else will do! Or lamb or veal or pork, for that matter. These recipes are exquisitely flavored, complex yet simple, and again, like so many other recipes in this book, better if they are done the day before and reheated. Please note that even if these recipes have many steps, none is particularly complicated, and always remember that the extra small step is, more often than not, what separates the extraordinary from the ordinary!

OPPOSITE *Perfect Roast Tenderloin of Beef just out of the oven*

Perfect Roast Tenderloin of Beef with Horseradish Sauce

A COUPLE of years ago, Dennis Hopper received a star on the Hollywood Walk of Fame. I hosted a lunch for him, his family, and his friends afterwards, and when I asked him what he would like for lunch, he answered, without hesitation, "Beef!" There were 120 of us, and it was a buffet, so I served Marinated Shrimp (page 28) and Dorothy's Fried Chicken (page 203) also, but Dennis's favorite was this roast tenderloin of beef. He told me it was the very best one he had ever had.

YIELD: *One 6- to 8-pound tenderloin, 10 to 12 servings*

1 (6- to 8-pound) beef tenderloin, trimmed of its silver skin

2 teaspoons salt

1 teaspoon ground black pepper

2 tablespoons dried thyme

1 stick (8 tablespoons) salted butter, softened

2 tablespoons finely minced garlic

3 tablespoons finely chopped shallots

Preheat the oven to broil.

Rub both sides of the tenderloin generously with the salt, pepper, and thyme.

In a small bowl, combine the butter, garlic, and shallots, and mash them with a fork. Rub the composed butter, generously, on top of the tenderloin, and then put it on a metal baking pan. Place the baking pan on the middle rack of the preheated oven and broil the tenderloin, butter side up, for exactly 5 minutes.

Turn the oven down to 400°F.

Roast the tenderloin for 17 minutes more.

Turn the oven again to broil, and broil the tenderloin for an additional 2 minutes. Remove it from the oven.

Let the beef rest for at least 12 to 15 minutes before slicing. Serve it warm or cold.

After you season the tenderloin on both sides with the salt, pepper, and dried thyme, spread the composed butter on top.

Erlinda's Exquisite Short Ribs

NOT ONLY is Erlinda exquisite, so are her short ribs. After thirty years as head chef for my friend Betsy Bloomingdale in Los Angeles, she moved back to the Philippines. Betsy keeps a diary of what dishes she has served to which guests, and tries never to repeat her selections, but I requested these ribs so many times that it became a running joke. Before Erlinda left, I asked her to write down the recipe for me. Like most good cooks, she used a written recipe merely as a springboard for creativity, so much of what you see here is my extrapolation. These are superlative in every way, easy enough, and one of those slow-cooked, falling-off-the-bone luscious, moments more delicious than any I have ever tasted.

(continued on next page)

Happy times: Betsy Bloomingdale, Oscar de la Renta, and Princess Ira von Fürstenberg, New York, circa 1982

OPPOSITE *Here's how brown and crusty the ribs should be!*

(continued from previous page)

YIELD: *8 servings (about 2 ribs per person)*

3 pounds beef short ribs, cut into
2-inch pieces at right angles to
the bone
1 teaspoon salt, divided
¾ teaspoon ground black pepper,
divided
5 tablespoons flour
4 tablespoons salted butter, divided
2 tablespoons vegetable oil

3 cups chopped onion
½ cup diced carrots
½ cup diced celery
2¼ cups red wine
3 cups chicken stock
¼ teaspoon dried thyme
1 bay leaf
2 tablespoons chopped parsley

Preheat the oven to 350°F.

Season both sides of the short ribs with ½ teaspoon of the salt (¼ teaspoon per side) and ½ teaspoon of the black pepper.

Place the flour in a medium mixing bowl and toss the seasoned ribs in the flour until they are coated. Shake off the excess flour and reserve the ribs.

In a large, heavy skillet over medium-high heat, melt 2 tablespoons of the butter with the oil. When the foaming has subsided, add the ribs.

This is the most crucial step: brown, and I mean brown, the ribs in the butter and oil on all sides until they are crusty, about 15 to 20 minutes. You may have to do this in batches. Do not crowd the pan, or you will steam the meat instead of browning it. Pay attention, as this is truly the most important step in making this dish. Transfer the browned ribs to a 13 × 9 × 2-inch baking dish and let them cool.

Remove the burned oil and butter from the skillet, and let the skillet cool slightly.

Melt the remaining 2 tablespoons butter in the skillet over low heat, but do not let the butter burn. The skillet will be very hot.

When the foaming has subsided, add the onions and sauté them for about 2 minutes, until they are just slightly translucent, and then add the carrots and celery. Sauté them for approximately 10 to 12 minutes more, until the vegetables are just barely soft.

Add the cooked vegetables to the baking dish with the ribs, and then pour in the wine and stock. Add the remaining ½ teaspoon salt and ¼ teaspoon black pepper, and the thyme. Top the dish with a bay leaf in the middle.

Cover the baking dish tightly with aluminum foil and bake it for 2½ hours.

Remove it from the oven, uncover it, and take out the bay leaf. Remove the meat and pour the liquid and vegetables into a heavy medium saucepan. Place the saucepan in the freezer for about 20 minutes, and then skim off the excess fat. Reduce the oven to 300°F.

After you have skimmed the fat, place the saucepan on the stove over high heat and boil until the sauce thickens, 8 to 10 minutes. Add the parsley.

Put the ribs back in the baking dish and pour half the thickened sauce over them. Cover the dish tightly and put it in the oven again for 1 more hour. Remove the ribs and uncover them. They should be falling off the bone by now. Heat the rest of the sauce in a heavy saucepan over a medium heat.

Turn the oven to broil. Broil the ribs for 5 to 7 minutes, until caramelized, and then let them rest for about 5 minutes before serving. Pass the remaining sauce with the ribs when it's time to serve them.

NOTE These are *infinitely* better if all the steps up to the broiling are done the day before serving.

Billionaire's Meatloaf

CASEY RIBICOFF, the widow of the former Connecticut governor and Kennedy cabinet member Abraham Ribicoff, and a confidante of Bill Blass, Dominick Dunne, Barbara Walters, and Nancy Kissinger alike, became my friend when I first moved to New York, and very early on I went to a dinner at her Sutton Place apartment that I will never forget. Casey was a game dame and an excellent hostess. This dinner was the epitome of the high-low juxtaposition, one that I find to be totally appealing. Passed with drinks, there was nothing but the very best French foie gras. The first course was exquisite smoked salmon and Beluga caviar, both served with every imaginable accompaniment. It was truly over the top. The main course was meatloaf, mashed potatoes, and peas. You get the point. I loved the humor and restraint that showed, and the more high-flown one of my courses might be, I always try to have a classic comfort dish as another. Nothing embodies comfort food like meatloaf.

YIELD: *8 servings*

4 tablespoons salted butter

2½ cups chopped onion

4 tablespoons minced shallots

1 pound sliced mushrooms

1 tablespoon salt plus ½ teaspoon salt, divided

2 tablespoons brandy

2 large eggs

1 pound ground beef chuck, at room temperature

1 pound ground pork, at room temperature

1 pound ground lamb, at room temperature

3 tablespoons Dijon mustard

1 tablespoon plus 1 teaspoon double-strength tomato paste

1 cup white bread crumbs, firmly packed

½ cup beef stock

1 cup grated mild Cheddar cheese, firmly packed

1 tablespoon minced garlic

1 teaspoon ground black pepper

¼ teaspoon cracked black pepper

2¼ teaspoons dried thyme

2 teaspoons paprika

1 teaspoon allspice

1½ teaspoons dried oregano

⅛ teaspoon minced dried bay leaf

2 slices par-cooked bacon for garnish

Preheat the oven to 375°F.

In a large, heavy skillet over medium heat, melt the butter. When the foaming has subsided, add the onions and shallots and sauté them for 2 minutes, until just soft.

Add the mushrooms, ½ teaspoon of the salt, and the brandy, and sauté for another 2 minutes, until just soft. Remove from the heat.

Beat the eggs in a large mixing bowl. Add the beef, pork, lamb, and the rest of the ingredients except the bacon.

Add the mushrooms and the onions, and all the cooking liquids from the pan. Knead the meat to combine, but do not mix it too much or it will be tough.

Free-form the meat mixture into a loaflike shape on a heavy baking sheet or place it in a buttered loaf pan and "bang" it on the bottom to deflate the air bubbles. Place the par-cooked bacon in a cross on top and bake for 1½ hours, until the internal temperature has reached no higher than 155°F. It may be helpful for you to use a meat thermometer for this, but make sure you add it before the meat cooks. Do not poke the cooked meat with a thermometer or all of the juices will run out. Let the meatloaf rest for at least 15 minutes before you slice it and serve it.

First nighters: Abe and Casey Ribicoff at the opening of the American Ballet Theater, New York, 1991

Osso Buco

A COUPLE of years ago in Los Angeles there seemed to be an osso buco lollapalooza. There were two dinners, Betsy Bloomingdale's and mine, and one lunch, given by Prince and Princess Rupert Loewenstein (he's the business mastermind behind the Rolling Stones). In the course of about ten days, we all got our fill of osso buco. This recipe is the combination of the best elements of all three of those dishes. It's good to serve this dish in the winter when there is a chill in the evening air.

YIELD: *8 servings*

3 pounds veal shanks with bones
1 teaspoon salt, divided
½ teaspoon ground black pepper, divided
5 tablespoons flour
4 tablespoons salted butter, divided
2 tablespoons vegetable oil
3 cups chopped onion
1 cup sliced onions

½ cup diced carrots
½ cup diced celery
2¼ cups red wine
3½ cups chicken stock
¼ teaspoon dried thyme
1 bay leaf
2 tablespoons chopped parsley
Gremolata (recipe follows)

Preheat the oven to 350°F.

Season both sides of the veal shanks with ½ teaspoon of the salt and ¼ teaspoon of the black pepper.

Place the flour in a medium mixing bowl and toss the seasoned shanks in the flour until they are coated. Shake off the excess flour and reserve the ribs.

In a large, heavy skillet over medium-high heat, melt 2 tablespoons of the butter with the oil. When the foaming has subsided, add the shanks to the skillet.

This is the most crucial step: brown, and I mean brown, the shanks in the butter and oil on all sides until they are crusty, 15 to 20 minutes. You may have to do this in batches. Do not crowd the pan, or you will steam the meat instead of browning it. Pay attention, as this is truly the most important part of this recipe. Transfer the browned shanks to a 13 × 9 × 2-inch baking dish and let them cool.

Remove the burned oil and butter from the skillet, and let the skillet cool slightly.

Melt the remaining 2 tablespoons butter in the skillet over low heat, but do not let the butter burn. The skillet will be very hot.

When the foaming has subsided, add both the sliced and chopped onions and sauté for about 2 minutes, until just slightly translucent, and then add the carrots and celery. Sauté for 10 to 12 minutes, until the vegetables are just barely soft.

Transfer the cooked vegetables to the baking dish with the shanks, and then pour in the wine and stock. Add the remaining ½ teaspoon salt and ¼ teaspoon black pepper, and the thyme. Top the dish with a bay leaf in the middle.

Cover the baking dish tightly and bake for 2½ hours.

Remove it from the oven, uncover it, and remove the bay leaf. Remove the meat and pour the liquid and vegetables into a heavy medium saucepan. Place the saucepan in the freezer for about 20 minutes, and then skim off the excess fat. Reduce the oven heat to 300°F.

After you have skimmed the fat, place the saucepan on the stove over high heat and boil until the sauce thickens, 8 to 10 minutes. Add the parsley.

Put the shanks back in the baking dish and pour half the thickened sauce over them. Cover the dish tightly and put it in the oven again for 45 minutes to 1 hour. Remove the shanks and uncover them. They should be falling off the bone by now. Heat the rest of the sauce in a heavy saucepan over medium heat.

Turn the oven to broil. Broil the shanks for 5 to 7 minutes, until they are caramelized, and then let them rest for about 5 minutes before serving. Top with the gremolata, and pass the remaining sauce with the shanks.

NOTE These are *infinitely* better if all the steps up to the broiling are done the day before serving.

Gremolata

2 tablespoons lemon zest	1 teaspoon olive oil
2 garlic cloves, peeled	½ teaspoon salt
4 sprigs parsley	¼ teaspoon ground black pepper

In the bowl of a food processor fitted with a metal blade, process all the ingredients until a paste forms. Serve the gremolata on top of the osso buco.

Seven-Hour Lamb

Gigot de Sept Heures

JAMES BEARD, who may be America's first famous foodie, and who really needs no introduction in the food world as his tastes and standards are still very much alive at the James Beard Foundation, referred to this preparation as "spoon" lamb. It is so tender that you can eat it with a spoon. Even though it takes seven hours to cook, it is easy to prepare. I cannot say enough good things about this braised delicacy. I always serve it with Gratin Dauphinois (page 144) and usually in the early spring when it's still cold enough for one to appreciate such a full-flavored dish as this one.

YIELD: *8 servings*

1 (7- to 9-pound) leg of lamb, bone in
1 tablespoon salt
2 teaspoons ground black pepper
1½ teaspoons dried rosemary
1½ teaspoon dried thyme
1 bay leaf
½ cup olive oil
6 whole cloves

3 large onions, quartered
6 carrots, unpeeled and cut into ¾-inch slices
20 garlic cloves, peeled
1 (28-ounce) can whole tomatoes, drained
1½ cups red wine
2 cups beef stock

Preheat the oven to broil.

Season both sides of the lamb with the salt and pepper. Place it in a large roasting pan or baking dish. Scatter the rosemary, thyme, bay leaf, and olive oil over the lamb.

On the middle rack broil the lamb for 10 minutes. The lamb will be browned and charred in places.

Turn the oven down to 225°F.

Insert the cloves into half of the quartered onions and then dice the rest of the onions.

Add the carrots, garlic, tomatoes, wine, and stock to the lamb in the baking dish and cover it very tightly with multiple layers of aluminum foil.

Bake for 7 hours.

Remove the lamb from the oven and remove the cloves from the onions and discard them. Make sure you get all of the cloves out, or your dish will be ruined with too much clove flavor!

Pour the liquid off the lamb into a heavy saucepan and put it in the freezer for 20 minutes. Spoon all of the vegetables into the bowl of a food processor fitted with a metal blade and puree them. Remove the saucepan from the freezer and skim the fat away. Add the vegetables to the saucepan and, over high heat, boil until the flavors are concentrated and the liquid has reduced by about a third to a half, and pour it over the lamb. Serve tomorrow!

Culinary icons: James Beard, legendary Knopf editor Judith Jones, and Julia Child, early 1970s

Pulled Pork with Carolina Barbecue Sauce

THERE SEEMS to be a Southern food revival every several years. For me, of course, it never goes away. This dish is a classic, whether Southern food is in or out.

YIELD: *10 to 12 servings*

1 (7- to 9-pound) pork shoulder,
   bone in
1 tablespoon salt
1 teaspoon ground black pepper
1 pound carrots, coarsely chopped
1 pound onions, coarsely chopped
½ pound celery, coarsely chopped
1 branch rosemary

8 parsley sprigs
1 teaspoon dried thyme
4 cloves garlic
1½ teaspoons whole black
   peppercorns
3 quarts chicken stock
Carolina Barbecue Sauce
   (recipe follows)

Preheat the oven to 350°F.

Wash the pork, pat it dry, and place it in a deep metal roasting pan.

Season the meat with the salt and pepper and then add the carrots, onions, celery, rosemary, parsley, thyme, garlic, peppercorns, and stock to the pan.

Cover the pan tightly with foil in several layers so that there is no danger that the liquid will escape, and roast it for 5 to 5½ hours, until the pork is very tender.

Remove the foil and whatever small bit of fat there is, and "pull" the pork with two forks so that it is chunky and shredded. Place the pulled pork in a large container that can be covered in the refrigerator.

In a food processor fitted with a metal blade, puree all of the cooked vegetables and ¼ of the cooking liquid and then add it to the pulled pork. Add ⅔ of the Carolina barbecue sauce and reserve the remaining sauce.

Let the pork sit in the refrigerator, covered tightly, for 2 to 3 days.

When it's time to serve, place the pork in a large, heavy stockpot, add the remaining sauce, heat it slowly over medium-low heat until bubbling, and serve.

Carolina Barbecue Sauce

1½ pounds salted butter, melted
2½ cups apple cider vinegar
2½ cups red wine vinegar
¾ cup dry mustard
1⅞ cups Dijon mustard
2½ teaspoons celery seed

2 tablespoons salt
¾ cups minced garlic
1½ cups dark brown sugar
¾ cup lemon juice
2 teaspoons ground nutmeg

Heat all the ingredients in a medium heavy saucepan over medium heat. Stir the sauce until the sugar melts, 5 to 7 minutes. Do not let the sauce boil.

Broccoli Slaw (page 66) is always right with Pulled Pork with Carolina Barbecue Sauce.

Roasted Pork Tenderloin
with Cilantro Lime Butter

ALTHOUGH THE instructions here are for the oven, this pork tenderloin would be just as happy on the grill, seared to perfection. It is amazing either way. I love to serve it with Caroline's Soubise (page 154) and Stewed Tomatoes (page 180) in the winter for dinner or, cold, in summer with Rice Salad (page 92). I find that, for this dish, I always end up preparing more than one tenderloin, and the leftovers are fantastic, if they ever dare to get that far.

YIELD: *One (1- to 1½-pound) tenderloin, about 4 servings*

1 (1- to 1½-pound) pork tenderloin
Pork Rub (recipe follows)

Cilantro Lime Butter (recipe follows)

Preheat the oven to 375°F.

Rinse and thoroughly pat dry the pork tenderloin.

Coat the tenderloin on all sides with the pork rub and then smear 8 tablespoons of the cilantro lime butter on top.

Place the pork loin on a metal baking sheet and roast it for 22 to 25 minutes, until the internal temperature of the pork is at least 140°F. There should be no more pinkness to the meat.

Let the tenderloin rest for at least 5 minutes, spread the remaining cilantro lime butter on top, slice, and serve.

Pork Rub

(for 1 to 1½ pounds of tenderloin)

2 bay leaves, de-stemmed
1 teaspoon dried thyme
2 teaspoons salt

1 teaspoon ground black pepper
2 tablespoons minced garlic

Combine all the ingredients in the bowl of a food processor fitted with a metal blade and puree thoroughly. Reserve.

Spooning Cilantro Lime Butter over Roasted Pork Tenderloin, which I sometimes serve with Orange Mayonnaise (page 128)

Cilantro Lime Butter

YIELD: *6 ounces (12 tablespoons)*

1 stick (8 tablespoons) salted butter
2 tablespoons fresh lime juice
1 garlic clove, peeled
1 medium shallot, peeled
Zest of one medium lime

3 tablespoons cilantro leaves
¼ teaspoon whole black peppercorns
½ teaspoon salt
¼ teaspoon ground black pepper

Combine all the ingredients in the bowl of a food processor fitted with a metal blade, and puree thoroughly until the garlic, shallots, cilantro, and peppercorns are fully chopped. Reserve.

Bread is the warmest, kindest of words;

write it always with a capital letter,

like your own name.

ANONYMOUS

10

Biscuits, Rolls, Breads, Pastry, and Crêpes

In this chapter, I explore the iconic Southern biscuit and its variations, but you will also find very traditional Southern staples like Yeast Rolls (page 262) and Sally Lunn Bread (page 265), all updated to pass the flavor and quality tests of today. Some of these traditional recipes you may not find in any other books being published now. When I was growing up, we often had a hot quick bread or yeast rolls at dinner, made by Dorothy that afternoon, and they were so good that I want to share them with you. I do not use any of her bread recipes or pie crusts here, as they all had shortening in them, but I have updated and re-created the ideas where I could, and am pleased to serve them up, hot, to the foodies we have all become!

OPPOSITE *Preparing Pâte Brisée (page 268)*

Perfect Biscuits and Variations

IN DEVELOPING what I consider to be the perfect biscuit, I started by researching what must be every book ever written on biscuits, and read literally hundreds of recipes, each one differing ever so slightly. I tested and retested recipes from distinguished authorities and venerated volumes: Bill Neal, Edna Lewis, Mrs. S. R. Dull, *Charleston Receipts, Joy of Cooking, Cook's Illustrated* (which has a very unorthodox but delicious whipping-cream biscuit), with themes and variations like cream-cheese biscuits, buttermilk biscuits, beaten biscuits, herb biscuits, cheese biscuits, and on and on. After making hundreds of versions of the Southern biscuit, I came up with the formula that I thought was the best and one that eschewed both shortening and buttermilk. My sweet-milk biscuit is made of pure butter and can serve as an all-purpose base for ham, herbs, and cheese; as a crust for savory chicken and salmon pot pies; and, by the addition of more sugar, as a topping for sweet fruit cobblers.

YIELD: *18 to 24 biscuits*

2 cups all-purpose flour
½ teaspoon sugar
1¼ teaspoons salt
1⅛ tablespoons baking powder
  (make sure it's new!)

1 stick (8 tablespoons) salted butter,
  cold and cut into quarters
¾ cup cold milk
Egg wash: 1 beaten egg plus
  1 tablespoon heavy cream

Preheat the oven to 450°F.

Combine the flour, sugar, salt, and baking powder in the bowl of a food processor fitted with a metal blade, and pulse it a couple of times until it is fully combined.

Add the cold butter, all at once, and pulse it until it resembles coarse crumbs, 8 to 10 times.

Pour the milk through the feed tube, slowly, while pulsing, until the milk is completely added. This will take 20 to 25 pulses. Pea-size crumbs will form. Do not continue pulsing until the dough pulls away from the sides of the bowl, or the biscuits will be tough.

Pour the pea-size crumbs onto a floured surface, and add fresh herbs or other ingredients (see variations) if desired.

(continued on next page)

(continued from previous page)

Gather the crumbs together, kneading 2 to 3 times. Do not overknead the dough, or the biscuits will be tough.

Roll the dough out to ¼- to ½-inch thickness, and cut with whatever size biscuit cutter you like.

Place the biscuits on a heavy baking sheet so that they are touching each other on all sides to facilitate rising, and brush generously with the egg wash.

Bake for 8 to 10 minutes, until golden brown on top.

These biscuits are delicious plain, split, buttered, and toasted, just as Merle is doing here, but get creative if you like!

Cheddar Biscuits

To the Perfect Biscuits recipe, after pouring the pea-size crumbs onto a floured surface, add:

¼ cup diced sharp Cheddar cheese   ⅛ teaspoon cayenne pepper

Chive Biscuits

To the Perfect Biscuits recipe, after pouring the pea-size crumbs onto a floured surface, add:

3 tablespoons chopped fresh chives

Herb Biscuits

To the Perfect Biscuits recipe, after pouring the pea-size crumbs onto a floured surface, add:

2 tablespoons chopped fresh dill   2 tablespoons chopped fresh basil
1 tablespoon chopped fresh parsley

Ham and Cheese Biscuits

After the Perfect Biscuits are finished and cooled, slice them in half, brush them with melted butter, and make a mini-sandwich by adding prosciutto or country ham and some sharp Cheddar cheese, and reheat them until the cheese is slightly melted.

Yeast Rolls

THESE ARE one of my absolute favorite things. Growing up, I always knew it was time for a party when yeast rolls appeared, often to accompany a beef tenderloin and either béarnaise sauce or horseradish sauce. I love them toasted with butter, but then, I guess most everything is better toasted with butter.

YIELD: *40 to 50 rolls*

2 cups whole milk
4 tablespoons salted butter
4 tablespoons sugar
2½ teaspoons salt
2 packages active dry yeast
    (make sure it's new!)

¼ cup lukewarm water (110°–115°F)
5 cups flour
Melted butter for brushing

In a medium saucepan over medium heat, bring the milk to a simmer, add the butter, sugar, and salt, turn off the heat, and let it stand until it has cooled to lukewarm. In another bowl, combine the yeast and the lukewarm water. If the water is too cool, the yeast will not activate; and if it's too hot, it will kill the yeast. After about 5 minutes or so, you will see the yeast begin to bubble. If you do not see it bubble, it's dead, so throw it away and start over with a new package of yeast.

In a large mixing bowl, combine the yeast, once it has dissolved, and the warm milk mixture and stir. Add the flour and stir the mixture gently to make a soft dough.

Turn the dough out onto a lightly floured board and let it rest for 10 minutes.

Place the dough in the bowl of an electric stand mixer with the dough hook attached, and turn the mixer on low to knead the dough for 3 minutes.

Brush the inside of a large mixing bowl with melted butter and add the dough. Cover the bowl and set it in the warmest place in your kitchen and let it rise for approximately 1½ to 2 hours.

Punch the dough down with your fist 1 to 2 times to deflate it.

Turn the dough out onto a floured surface and roll it out to ½-inch thickness.

Cut the dough with a medium biscuit cutter and place it on a heavy metal baking sheet. Brush the rounds generously with melted butter, and then fold them over in half and brush the tops generously with melted butter. Cover the unbaked rolls and put it in the warmest place in your kitchen and let it rise again for 2 hours.

Preheat the oven to 375°F, and bake the rolls, after they have risen the second time, for 10 minutes, until they are golden brown. Serve them immediately.

Sally Lunn Bread

THIS IS another indigenous Southern treat, whose origins are somewhat unclear. In the eighteenth century, according to lore, there may or may not have been an actual Sally Lunn and she may or may not have been English, but it really doesn't matter. This is the South's answer to brioche: yeasty, buttery, light and airy, and incredibly easy, as it requires no kneading whatsoever. In fact, this may be the easiest bread recipe of all time, and you'll have such a feeling of accomplishment when you serve it; it is a big tube-shaped loaf, as impressive in its presentation as it is in its exquisite flavor.

YIELD: *1 loaf, about 16 servings*

1½ cups milk

¼ cup sugar

1 (¼-ounce) package active dry yeast (make sure it's new!)

1 tablespoon salt

3 eggs, at room temperature, beaten

1 stick (8 tablespoons) salted butter, melted, plus more for brushing

5½ cups all-purpose flour, plus more for the pan

In a medium saucepan over medium heat, heat the milk until it is lukewarm (110°–115°F). Milk that is too hot will kill the yeast; milk that is too cool will not activate the yeast.

In a large mixing bowl, combine the lukewarm milk and sugar. Shake the dry yeast over it, and wait up to 5 minutes until you see a slight bubbling. If there is no bubbling, discard the mixture, buy new yeast, and start again.

To the bubbling mixture, add the salt, beaten eggs, 8 tablespoons melted butter, and 3 cups of the flour. Stir gently, but do not overmix it or the bread will be tough.

Add the remaining 2½ cups flour to the bowl, stirring gently to form a soft dough. Do not knead this dough. Brush the inside of a large mixing bowl with melted butter and add the dough. Cover it and set it in the warmest place in your kitchen and allow it to rise for 1 to 2 hours, until it has doubled in size. After the dough has doubled in size, preheat the oven to 375°F, and butter and flour a 10-inch tube pan or bundt mold.

Punch the dough down with your fist, once or twice, to deflate it, and spoon it into the prepared pan. Cover the dough, set it in the warmest place in your kitchen, and let it rise for another 1 to 2 hours, until it has doubled again in size.

(continued on next page)

(continued from previous page)

Brush the top with melted butter and bake it for 25 to 30 minutes, until it is golden brown.

Let it cool for 10 minutes, run the dull edge of a knife around the outside of the pan, and invert it onto a platter to release the bread. Let it cool for 15 to 20 minutes, then slice and serve it. Or slice it, toast it, and butter it, and then serve it.

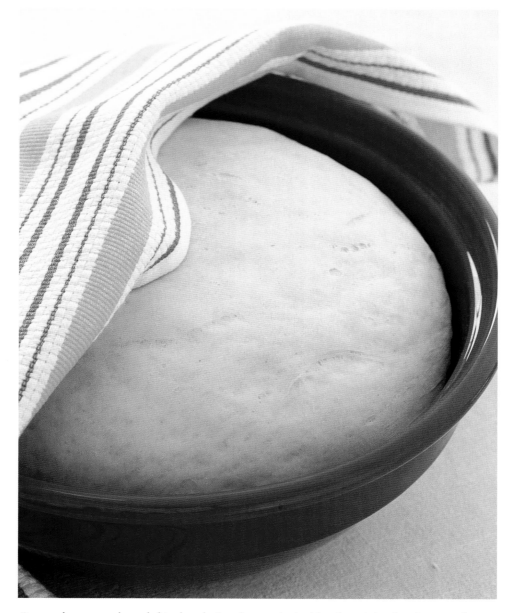

Remember not to knead this dough. Just butter the inside of a mixing bowl, cover the dough, and let it rise in the warmest place in your kitchen. Easy enough, right?

Crisp Yet Creamy Corn Muffins

I NEVER really liked corn bread until these came along. These muffins are fantastic, and notice that they are not made with the bacon grease so many corn breads in the South are. Yuck! These are crisp on the outside, creamy on the inside, delicately flavored, and a welcome partner for Pulled Pork with Carolina Barbecue Sauce (page 250), Broccoli Slaw (page 66), and Stewed Tomatoes (page 180).

YIELD: *48 small muffins or 16 regular muffins*

Butter for the muffin tins, plus
　　2 tablespoons salted butter
2 cups corn (fresh off the cob or
　　frozen)
2 cups yellow cornmeal
2 cups flour
½ cup sugar

1 tablespoon salt
2 tablespoons baking powder
3 cups heavy cream
1 stick (8 tablespoons) salted butter,
　　melted
4 eggs, at room temperature

Preheat the oven to 325°F. Butter whatever size muffin tins you like.

In a medium heavy skillet over medium heat, melt the 2 tablespoons butter. When the foaming has subsided, add the corn and sauté it until it just starts to soften. Turn off the heat and reserve the corn.

Whisk together the cornmeal, flour, sugar, salt, and baking powder in a large mixing bowl.

Add the cream and melted butter and stir until combined.

Beat the eggs in the bowl of an electric stand mixer fitted with the whisk attachment, on medium-high speed, until they are very light and have tripled in volume, about 5 minutes.

Gently fold the beaten eggs into the cornmeal mixture, and then add the sautéed corn.

Spoon the batter into the muffin tins and bake the muffins for about 15 minutes until they are crisp on the outside, yet still creamy in the middle. Serve immediately.

Basic Crêpes
(to be filled with anything)

THESE DELICATE crêpes are so easy you will wonder why you never made them before. I fill them with My Smoked Salmon Tartare (page 24), and top them with a Beurre Blanc (page 136), and then reheat them for serving. Please experiment with fillings as you wish. As delicate as these are, they are also very durable, and may be done days ahead and then filled when it's time to serve.

YIELD: *About 8 crêpes*

2 large eggs
¾ cup milk
½ cup water
1 cup flour

3 tablespoons salted butter, melted
¼ teaspoon salt
¼ cup chopped fresh herbs (optional)

Put all the ingredients in a blender and pulse them together 10 times. Refrigerate the batter for at least 1 hour.

Heat a 10-inch nonstick crêpe pan over high heat until it is hot all the way through. When the pan is hot, pour in ¼ cup of the crêpe batter and let it cook for 40 to 60 seconds until it is set on the bottom and bubbly on the top. Remove the crêpe from the pan and set it aside. Repeat this step until the batter is exhausted.

Variation

Optional for sweet crêpes: add 2½ tablespoons sugar, 1 teaspoon vanilla extract, 2 tablespoons any liqueur, and follow the same instructions.

NOTE These crêpes will keep in your refrigerator for at least a week, so you can do them ahead and fill them later.

These crepes can be done days ahead and later stuffed with, in this instance, My Smoked Salmon Tartare (page 24).

11

Desserts

Whenever I allow myself to taste sweets, I have a profound sweet tooth. Here's my issue with desserts: I find most of them just not very good, and certainly not worth the calories. Often they are made with inferior ingredients. In this chapter, I have tried to change all that. My guarantee: every single one of these confections is worth the calories. They are unusual, unexpected, and truly scrumptious. I won't suggest that dessert is health food. When I was testing recipes for this chapter, I found the more dessert I ate, the more I wanted to eat, and two things happened. These recipes fell into the CSE (Can't Stop Eating . . .) category and, subsequently, I popped out in places that my trainer is bound and determined to have pop back in. We are on the way. My advice: enjoy them, as you should, but just don't make all of these desserts at one time!

Almond Raspberry White Chocolate Bars

I'LL CHALLENGE you to taste anything better. These three flavors together on top of a shortbread crust are simply amazing. And, to boot, these bars are truly convenient. Along with my Priceless Pecan Bars (page 312), Luscious Lemon-Ginger Squares (page 307), and Best-Ever Brownies (page 283), these sinful treats can be made weeks ahead of time and frozen until it's time to serve them. As an added bonus, they all cut much better when they are frozen, and none of them take much time to thaw. They make perfect desserts for my buffets, passed in tandem with each other or alone. I cut these in "fingers," a small rectangular shape that is large enough to fully get the flavor of these confections but not large enough to tip the scales unfavorably unless you get greedy. (Note: I wouldn't hold it against you if you did.)

YIELD: *One 13 x 9 x 2-inch pan, 28 to 32 finger desserts*

CRUST

2 sticks (16 tablespoons) salted butter, cold and cut into small pieces, plus more for the baking pan

½ cup powdered sugar
1¾ cups all-purpose flour
¾ teaspoon almond extract
¼ teaspoon vanilla extract
¼ teaspoon salt

Preheat the oven to 350°F. Butter a 9 x 13 x 2-inch metal baking pan.

In the bowl of an electric mixer fitted with the paddle attachment, mix all of the ingredients slowly until coarse crumbs form.

Press the crumbs into the bottom of the prepared baking pan, and bake the crust for 25 minutes, until it is golden brown and completely cooked through. Remove it from the oven and let it cool completely.

TOPPING

½ teaspoon salt
½ cup sliced raw almonds

1¼ cups seedless raspberry jam
12 ounces white chocolate chips

In a small mixing bowl, toss the salt and almonds together.

Spread the jam evenly over the cooled crust, then add the white chocolate chips, and top with the salted almonds.

Bake the bars for 20 minutes, remove them from the oven, and let cool.

I always pass Almond Raspberry White Chocolate Bars on this small tray after big buffets.

Apple and Pear Crumble
with Maple Cinnamon Ice Cream

I HAVE never really liked apples. Yes, I would accept a bite of someone's tarte tatin, but rarely did it change my life. I feel unpatriotic to say that I do not like apple pie, but, then again, I may not like what an inferior product it has become. This apple and pear crumble makes my apple phobia disappear.

YIELD: *One 13 × 9 × 2-inch baking dish, 10 to 12 servings*

APPLE-PEAR MEDLEY

6 tablespoons salted butter

2 pounds apples, cored, peeled, sliced

1 pound pears, cored, peeled, sliced

1 cup dark brown sugar,
    firmly packed

¾ cup sugar

¾ teaspoon salt

½ cup Calvados

½ teaspoon cinnamon

½ teaspoon nutmeg

½ teaspoon allspice

2 teaspoons lemon juice

3 tablespoons flour

CRUMB CRUST

¼ cup dark brown sugar,
    firmly packed

¾ cup sugar

2¼ cups flour

¾ cups rolled oats

1 teaspoon salt

2 tablespoons vanilla extract

22 tablespoons cold salted butter

Maple Cinnamon Ice Cream
    (recipe follows)

Preheat the oven to 375°F. Butter a 13 × 9 × 2-inch ceramic or glass baking dish. Peel and core the fruit.

In a large heavy skillet over a medium-high heat, melt the butter. When the foaming has subsided, add the apples and the pears and sauté them for 2 to 3 minutes, until they just begin to get soft. Add the dark brown sugar, sugar, salt, Calvados, cinnamon, nutmeg, allspice, and lemon juice and continue to sauté for approximately 8 to 10 more minutes, until the sauce is a thick, rich caramel and the apples and pears are fully soft.

Add the flour and stir to incorporate it thoroughly. Sauté for another 2 minutes, then turn off the heat and set the apples and pears aside.

To make the crumb crust, in a large mixing bowl combine the dark brown sugar, sugar, flour, rolled oats, and salt, and whisk them together until they are blended. Add the vanilla and mix well.

Cut the butter into the dry mixture with a pastry cutter until coarse crumbs form.

Pour the apple-pear medley into the prepared baking dish, and generously spread the crumbs on top.

Bake for 30 minutes, until the crust is brown and the sauce is bubbling, remove it from the oven, and serve it warm with the maple cinnamon ice cream.

Maple Cinnamon Ice Cream

YIELD: *2 quarts (how many that serves is up to you because some people, like me, could eat the entire thing)*

2 eggs

1¼ cups sugar

6 tablespoons pure maple syrup

1 tablespoon vanilla extract

1¼ teaspoons cinnamon

¼ teaspoon salt

2 cups heavy cream

2 cups milk

In the bowl of an electric stand mixer fitted with the whisk attachment, beat the eggs and sugar together on medium-high speed until they are light, approximately 5 minutes.

Prepare a double boiler. Over medium heat, cook the eggs and sugar in the top of the double boiler until they have just thickened, stirring them often. Remove them from the heat and add the maple syrup, vanilla, cinnamon, salt, heavy cream, and milk. Freeze the mixture in an ice cream freezer according to the manufacturer's directions.

Peggy's Apricot Mousse: A Faux Soufflé

THIS DESSERT was one of my seminal food moments. Let's go to 1979, and the Atlanta kitchen of my cousin Peggy Foreman, a self-taught, locally renowned chef who taught cooking classes to Atlanta's gratin long before food was fashionable. She and her husband, Rawson, are charming, popular, and civically active; he is, among many other things, the former chairman of Atlanta's High Museum of Art, and she is a culinary guru-cum-businesswoman. They entertained often, and exquisitely, in their chic David Hicks–inspired house. There was always serious, impeccable food and generations of ornate family silver set against the lightness of David Hockney's limpid pools or one of Magritte's tomatoes on their walls. It was at one of their weekly Saturday dinners, about which *Southern Accents* magazine did an early lifestyle story, that this dessert cropped up. I will never forget it, and have never had another apricot dish that approaches it since. I went home and told my mother, who called Peggy. The recipe came along soon thereafter, and it became a staple in our house.

Peggy has been instrumental in the testing of the recipes for this book and her generosity shows through page after page. She doesn't always agree with me, and when this happens she invariably says, "Well, that's what makes a horse race!" She's right. This recipe is completely hers, not mine. How I wish I could claim authorship. The only thing that I can claim is undying love and gratitude for Rawson, Peggy, their children, and last, but not least, this amazing apricot mousse!

YIELD: *8 servings*

2 cups dried apricots
2 cups water
2 cups sugar, divided
Juice and zest of 2 lemons, plus
    6 tablespoons lemon juice,
    divided

3 egg yolks
1 teaspoon vanilla extract
½ teaspoon salt
1 cup heavy cream
6 egg whites

In a heavy medium-sized sauce pan over a medium-low heat, simmer together the apricots, water, 1 cup of the sugar, and the juice and zest of 2 lemons, for

(continued on next page)

(continued from previous page)

about 30 minutes, until the fruit is very soft. Remove from the heat and allow the fruit to cool for 30 to 45 minutes in the cooking liquid.

Drain the apricots in a colander, but reserve 1 cup of the cooking liquid.

In the bowl of a food processor fitted with a metal blade, combine the cooked apricots, the remaining 6 tablespoons lemon juice, and the reserved cooking liquid. Puree the apricots until they are very smooth, approximately 3 to 4 minutes.

In the bowl of an electric stand mixer fitted with the whisk attachment, beat together the egg yolks, the remaining cup of sugar, the vanilla, and salt for about 5 minutes on medium speed, until the mixture is very light in color.

Add the pureed apricot, and continue beating for another 5 minutes.

Whip the cream until soft peaks form, and fold the whipped cream into the apricot and egg mixture.

Beat the egg whites until stiff peaks form, and gently fold the beaten whites into the mixture.

Make an aluminum collar for a 4-cup soufflé dish. Pour the mousse into the soufflé dish and freeze it overnight.

Uncollar it and serve.

New Orleans Bread Pudding with Vanilla Bourbon Sauce

BACK TO New Orleans again, this time to the world-famous Commander's Palace, a rambling restaurant in the Garden District described as "[a] turquoise and white Victorian fantasy of a building complete with turrets, columns, and gingerbread, [which] has been known for the award-winning quality of its food and many commodious dining rooms since 1880." Now that we've gotten that out of the way, let's focus on what I believe to be the ultimate in bread puddings, Southern style. It was inspired by the one at Commander's Palace, but I have taken it to the limit, even if I do say so myself. See what you think. I doubt you'll be able to stop yourself.

YIELD: *3½ pounds, or one 13 × 9 × 2-inch baking dish*

½ pound good-quality white bread
4 eggs
2 cups sugar
2½ cups whole milk
6 tablespoons salted butter, melted
2 tablespoons bourbon
1⅛ teaspoons nutmeg
¾ teaspoon cinnamon

2¼ teaspoons vanilla extract
¼ teaspoon orange extract
2 tablespoons brown sugar
¾ cup golden raisins
¾ cup chopped pecans
¼ teaspoon salt
Vanilla Bourbon Sauce
    (recipe follows)

(continued on next page)

(continued from previous page)

Cut the bread into ½-inch cubes.

In the bowl of an electric mixer fitted with the whisk attachment on medium speed, beat the eggs and sugar together until they are light and fluffy, about 5 minutes.

Beat in the milk, melted butter, bourbon, nutmeg, cinnamon, and vanilla.

Place the bread in a 13 × 9 × 2-inch baking dish, and pour the liquid over the bread. Cover it and let it sit, refrigerated, for at least 3 hours, or preferably overnight.

When you're ready to bake, preheat the oven to 325°F.

Remove the baking dish from the refrigerator and stir in the orange extract, brown sugar, raisins, pecans, and salt, mixing thoroughly.

Bake the bread pudding for 40 minutes, until the custard has just set.

Serve it warm with the Vanilla Bourbon Sauce.

Vanilla Bourbon Sauce

Lee Bailey was a hero of mine. A Louisiana native, he spent his career in New York as a home furnishings designer for the original ultra-stylish Henri Bendel store on West Fifty-seventh street, before he rediscovered his Southern food roots. He then wrote more books than the law allows, each more beautiful than the last. All of them made serving elegant food seem easy. He was the forefather of the "lifestyle" genre, and preached his gospel through sumptuous photographs of his friends' houses and their marvelous recipes. I knew Lee when I first arrived in New York, and never consider the combination of bourbon and vanilla without thinking of him and the sumptuous warm pecan pie over which he served a similarly delicious sauce.

YIELD: *2 cups*

2 cups heavy cream
1½ cups sugar
1 tablespoon vanilla extract

1 teaspoon salt
3 tablespoons bourbon

In a heavy saucepan over medium heat, whisk all the ingredients together, and slowly bring to a boil. Turn off the heat. Strain sauce through a fine sieve, and serve it warm or cold.

Best-Ever Brownies

DOROTHY HAD a "secret" brownie recipe, which I enjoyed all during my childhood and in care packages at boarding school and college. It was simple, and really good, but not like this one. Dorothy just took the *Joy of Cooking*'s basic recipe, and then doubled the butter. I loved those brownies but, sorry, Dorothy, they just weren't quite as good as these. The inspiration for these came from Ellen Hale Jones's family recipe, but I added more vanilla, more butter, and more salt, of all things, and I will put them up against any I have ever tasted. They are elegant, easy, and delicious—in short, everything we love.

YIELD: *28 to 32 brownies*

8 ounces unsweetened chocolate
24 tablespoons salted butter
4 cups sugar
6 eggs

1 tablespoon vanilla extract
2 cups flour
1 tablespoon plus ⅛ teaspoon salt

Preheat the oven to 350°F. Butter a 9 × 13-inch metal baking pan.

In a double boiler over low heat, melt the chocolate and the butter together.

Transfer the melted chocolate and butter to a large mixing bowl and stir in the sugar until it is well combined. Then add the eggs, vanilla, flour, and salt until they are just combined.

Pour the mixture into the prepared pan and bake the brownies for 32 to 35 minutes. Do not overbake them. They should be set, but still moving a tiny bit, and most seasoned brownie chefs would say that they are not quite done. They will be very soft and very difficult to handle, but completely worth it.

NOTE Be sure to mix these by hand, and not too much, as their texture will be gooier and fudgier the less uniform the batter is. I always do them ahead, freeze them, and cut them when they are frozen, as they are so much easier to handle.

Salted Caramel Cake

CARAMEL CAKE exists nowhere else that I know except the American South. It is the default go-to Special Occasion cake: birthdays, christenings, and funerals. So few people bake cakes anymore that it is not as prevalent as it once was, and what a shame that is. This cake is truly a treat, and well worth the effort. This cake is so good, I think you could probably sell it. Mark my words.

YIELD: *One 9-inch cake, approximately 16 servings*

CAKE

9 tablespoons salted butter, cold, plus more for the pans

3¼ cups plus 2 tablespoons sugar

2 tablespoons plus ¾ teaspoon vanilla extract

12 tablespoons salted butter, melted

8 egg yolks

4 eggs

3¾ cups cake flour, plus more for the pans

1 tablespoon plus 1½ teaspoons salt

1 tablespoon plus 1½ teaspoons baking powder

¾ cup buttermilk

1 cup plus 2 tablespoons heavy cream

Preheat the oven to 325°F. Butter and flour three 9-inch cake pans, put a parchment round in the bottom of each pan, and butter and flour the rounds.

In the bowl of an electric stand mixer fitted with the paddle attachment on medium-high speed, beat the cold butter until very light, about 5 minutes.

Scrape the bowl down several times while beating, and gradually add the sugar.

Add the vanilla and continue beating for 5 more minutes, scraping the bowl down again. The mixture will be very coarse and grainy.

Turn the speed to low and add the melted butter, egg yolks, and eggs, beating until they are fully combined. Turn off the mixer.

In a large mixing bowl, sift together the flour, salt, and baking powder.

In a medium mixing bowl, whisk together the buttermilk and cream, and then turn on the mixer again to the very lowest speed. Add half the flour, and then half the buttermilk mixture, and then the remaining flour, and then the remaining buttermilk mixture. Scrape down the bowl as necessary, but make sure not to overmix the batter, or the cake will be tough.

(continued on page 286)

(continued from page 284)

Pour the batter into the 3 prepared pans, dividing it equally, and bang each pan on a sturdy surface to release the air bubbles. Put the pans in the oven and bake them for 25 to 30 minutes, until they are brown on top and a toothpick or knife comes out clean.

Cool the cakes for 10 minutes, then run the dull edge of a knife around the perimeter of the pans and invert them onto a cold baking sheet or rack. Note: These cakes may be frozen for up to 3 months at this point.

When you are ready to ice the cake, slice each layer horizontally in half so that you will have 6 layers. Make sure all the layers are cold before you ice them.

CARAMEL ICING

4½ sticks (36 tablespoons) salted butter

1 cup plus 2 tablespoons half-and-half

4½ cups light brown sugar, firmly packed

2¼ cups powdered sugar, firmly packed

4 tablespoons vanilla extract

2¼ teaspoons salt

In a large heavy saucepan over medium heat, melt the butter. When the butter is fully melted, add the half-and-half, and then the brown sugar.

Turn the heat to high and bring the mixture to a boil. Reduce the heat and simmer for about 8 minutes, until the sugar is completely melted and the mixture is smooth.

Remove from the heat and let it cool to room temperature. I actually stick it in the freezer to cool for about 30 to 40 minutes because otherwise it could take all day.

When it's cool, transfer the caramel mixture to the bowl of an electric stand mixer fitted with the paddle attachment and, on medium speed, beat in the powdered sugar, vanilla, and salt.

Ice the cakes with about 1 cup of icing per layer. You may have a small bit of leftover icing, but this can easily be added to the top and sides.

Charlotte Russe

NOTHING SAYS Christmas Eve to me like Charlotte Russe. When I was growing up, we always had it, and its recipe was a time-honored family tradition. I have tweaked it a bit for today's palates, and the result is sensational. This cold, sherry-flavored unmolded custard with ladyfingers is undeniably old-fashioned, and I can guarantee that this cookbook is the only one that has come out recently with a recipe for it. These days, most people simply do not know what it is. What a pity!

YIELD: *8 to 10 servings*

2 tablespoons unflavored gelatin
½ cup cold water
2 cups half-and-half
1½ cups sugar
2 teaspoons flour
¾ teaspoon salt
8 egg yolks

1 tablespoon plus one teaspoon vanilla extract
¼ cup golden sherry
2 cups heavy cream
2 tablespoons powdered sugar
2 packages store-bought ladyfingers (18 to 24 fingers)

In a small bowl, dissolve the gelatin in the cold water until completely smooth, and set it aside.

In a heavy saucepan over medium heat, bring the half-and-half to a simmer.

In a large mixing bowl, whisk together the sugar, flour, and salt.

In an electric stand mixer fitted with the whisk attachment on medium speed, beat the egg yolks, and gradually add the flour mixture.

Pour the egg mixture into the warmed half-and-half, and stir it constantly until the mixture begins to thicken and coats the back of a spoon. Do not let it boil.

Remove it from the heat and strain it through a fine sieve into a large bowl. Stir in the vanilla, sherry, and dissolved gelatin.

Whip the heavy cream with the powdered sugar until soft peaks form.

When the egg and half-and-half mixture has cooled a bit and has set, and has basically the same consistency as the whipped cream, fold in the whipped cream.

Line a 10-cup charlotte mold (or a large upright bowl) with plastic wrap, and then generously with the ladyfingers in an attractive pattern.

Pour the custard into the mold and cover it. Refrigerate the custard overnight, until it is fully set, and then invert it onto a serving platter, remove the plastic wrap, and serve cold.

Crème Caramel

IT JUST doesn't get more classic than this. *Flan* in Spanish, this silky perfect custard topped with a salted caramel sauce is not nearly as popular now as its crystallized cousin Crème Brûlée, and I can't figure out why. It's easier to make, doesn't require any special equipment, and is a hit wherever/whenever. This recipe comes from The Patio by the River and, regardless of the season, was always on the menu. Don't pass up an opportunity to show off your abilities to your guests, and definitely do this a day or two ahead to allow the custard and caramel to set, and so you don't have any last-minute stress.

YIELD: *6-cups-plus caramel, enough to fill one 8-cup soufflé dish or two 4-cup soufflé dishes, to be unmolded*

CARAMEL
1 cup water
2 cups sugar
¼ teaspoon salt

CUSTARD
1 cup sugar
6 eggs
4 egg yolks
1 teaspoon vanilla extract
2 cups milk
2 cups cream
⅛ teaspoon salt

Preheat the oven to 325°F.

To make the caramel, heat 1 cup water with the sugar and the salt in a large heavy skillet over high heat until they boil. At this point, watch the mixture very carefully.

When it just becomes amber, or light golden brown, which could

(continued on next page)

OPPOSITE *Watch the caramel very carefully when it's cooking as it can burn quite quickly.* RIGHT *When it just begins to turn amber or light golden brown, immediately pour it into the soufflé dish.*

(continued from previous page)

take as long as 20 minutes, remove it from the heat and *immediately* pour it into an 8-cup soufflé dish or divide it equally in two 4-cup soufflé dishes.

To make the custard, whisk together the sugar, eggs, egg yolks, and vanilla until they are very light. Strain the egg mixture through a fine sieve and reserve it in a bowl.

Heat the milk and cream in a medium stockpot over medium heat. When it is thoroughly warm but not boiling, pour it into the strained egg mixture. Stir very well to combine.

Pour the custard mixture over the caramel in the soufflé dish(es) and assemble a bain-marie (see the note on page 169).

Place the soufflé dishes in the bain-marie and bake the crème caramel for 40 to 45 minutes, until just set but still trembling slightly.

Remove the crème caramel from the bain-marie and let cool. Cover them and refrigerate them overnight.

When it's time to serve, take the blunt edge of a knife and loosen the sides of the custard.

Invert the crème caramel onto a cold serving platter, letting the caramel run all over the top of the custard, and then serve.

Perfect Chocolate Chip Cookies

SEVERAL WINTERS ago in New York, there was a blizzard. I was between New York apartments and was staying with a friend. For what seemed like a week, we couldn't go out of the apartment, so what did we do? We made chocolate chip cookies, because those were the only ingredients that were on hand. After literally dozens of batches, these proportions are what I believe to be the perfect ones. They will not look like what you are accustomed to as they spread out while baking much more than their more traditional counterparts; they are elegant, thin, buttery, and irresistible.

YIELD: *16 to 24 cookies, depending on their size*

2 sticks (16 tablespoons) salted butter, softened

1 cup sugar

1 cup dark brown sugar, firmly packed

2 eggs

2 teaspoons vanilla extract

1½ cups flour

½ teaspoon baking soda

2½ teaspoons salt

1 (11- or 12-ounce) bag bittersweet chocolate chips

2 tablespoons grated orange zest

In the bowl of an electric mixer fitted with the whisk attachment on medium speed, cream the butter, sugar, and brown sugar together until they are light and fluffy, about 5 minutes.

Add the eggs one at a time, and then the vanilla. Scrape down the sides of the bowl.

In a separate bowl, whisk together the flour, baking soda, and salt, and with the mixer on the lowest speed, add it ½ cup at a time to the creamed butter and sugar until the dry ingredients are exhausted and the dough is just combined. Stir in the chocolate chips and orange zest and then refrigerate the dough for at least 1 hour.

Preheat the oven to 400°F and line a heavy baking sheet with parchment paper.

Place whatever size scoops of cold dough you desire on the prepared baking sheet, and bake the cookies for 10 to 15 minutes depending on their size. Let the cookies cool for at least 15 minutes before serving.

Molten Chocolate Cake

SINFUL, EASY, decadent, superb. Need I say anything else? It's the cake that needs no introduction! I serve this with Bourbon Whipped Cream (page 323) and raspberries or store-bought vanilla ice cream, or, if you are feeling creative, Maple Cinnamon Ice Cream (page 277). I also serve it alone. There is no way to go wrong. Unfortunately, you cannot do this ahead so make sure when you are serving it, you time things correctly. Too much baking, and it won't be molten anymore.

YIELD: *One 8-inch cake, 6 to 8 servings*

4 tablespoons salted butter, plus more for the pan

5 ounces semi-sweet chocolate, chopped

2 tablespoons Grand Marnier, or any other flavored liqueur

2 eggs, at room temperature

3 egg yolks, at room temperature

¾ cup sugar, plus more for the pan

1 teaspoon espresso powder

¼ teaspoon salt

1½ teaspoons vanilla extract

2 tablespoons flour

Preheat the oven to 375°F.

Butter an 8-inch heavy-gauge springform pan and dust it with sugar. This is an important part of this recipe, as one of the spectacular things here is the crust that is formed in this heavy metal pan from the butter and sugar.

In a heavy saucepan over very low heat, melt the butter and chocolate together, stirring constantly so as not to burn the chocolate.

Remove from the heat and stir in the Grand Marnier.

Beat the eggs and yolks in the bowl of an electric stand mixer fitted with the whisk attachment on medium speed, gradually adding the sugar, espresso powder, salt, and vanilla. Beat the mixture until it is very light, the "ribbon" (when the sugar falls back on itself like a ribbon!) forms, and the mixture has quadrupled in bulk. This should take between 7 and 10 minutes. Do not be impatient.

Sift the flour over the mixture, folding it in a little bit at a time, and then stir the chocolate into the egg mixture.

Pour the batter into the prepared springform pan and turn the oven down to 325°F. Bake the cake for 20 minutes, until a tender crust has formed, and then let it rest for 5 minutes before unmolding it and serving it hot.

Chocolate Mousse

HANDS DOWN, this is my favorite of all desserts, and the one, although I try never to serve my guests the same thing twice, I inevitably repeat. It's just that good. People literally go crazy over it, and once you master the steps, you can almost do it in your sleep. When it's time to serve it, I always put a layer of whipped cream on top and then garnish it with chopped and shaved chocolate.

YIELD: *6 to 8 servings*

8 egg yolks

1½ cups plus 2 tablespoons sugar, divided

⅛ teaspoon plus a pinch salt, divided

½ cup Grand Marnier or other orange liqueur

12 ounces semi-sweet chocolate

8 tablespoons very strong brewed coffee

3 sticks (24 tablespoons) salted butter, cold and cut into quarters

8 egg whites

In the bowl of an electric mixer fitted with the whisk attachment on medium speed, beat the egg yolks, 1½ cups of the sugar, ⅛ teaspoon of the salt, and the orange liqueur together, until the "ribbon" forms, about 5 minutes.

Prepare a double boiler, pour the egg yolk mixture into the top, and cook it over medium-low heat until it has just thickened, approximately 8 to 10 minutes. Do not overcook it or you will have scrambled eggs. Remove it from the heat and let cool slightly.

In a heavy, medium saucepan over very low heat, melt the chocolate with the coffee until they are smooth. Let them cool slightly.

In the bowl of an electric stand mixer fitted with the paddle attachment, combine the egg yolk mixture with the melted chocolate. With the mixer on medium speed, beat in the cold butter, adding a little at a time. Transfer the mixture to a large mixing bowl and reserve.

Wash the bowl of your electric mixer with cold water, so that the bowl is cold. Fit the mixer with the whisk attachment, and add the egg whites, the remaining 2 tablespoons sugar, and the remaining pinch salt and beat on medium speed until they stand in stiff peaks.

Stir about a quarter of the egg whites into the chocolate mixture and mix well to lighten the base.

Fold in the remaining egg whites and pour the mousse into a serving bowl. Do not smooth the mixture down as you do not want the egg whites to deflate.

Refrigerate the mousse overnight, and then serve.

Chocolate Soufflé
with Crème Anglaise

DESSERT SOUFFLÉ 101. Do yourself a favor and serve it at your next dinner party. It is a showstopper, and made even more fantastic by the crème anglaise that accompanies it. This version comes from esteemed chef Gail Monaghan, a New York friend who runs a popular cooking school. When I say 101, I truly mean it. It's one that she teaches to her legions of students, and I find it to be the best ever. Do yourself a favor: don't let the crème anglaise be relegated to rote chocolate soufflé use—it's an excellent addition to berries, mousses, and cakes alike.

YIELD: *6 to 8 servings*

Butter for the soufflé dish

8 ounces best-quality bittersweet chocolate, coarsely chopped

½ cup whole milk

⅔ cup plus ¼ cup sugar, plus more for the soufflé dish

1 teaspoon vanilla extract

¼ teaspoon salt

1 tablespoon espresso powder

6 egg yolks

8 egg whites, at room temperature

1 teaspoon cream of tartar

Powdered sugar for dusting

Créme Anglaise (recipe follows)

Preheat the oven to 400°F. Butter a 6-cup soufflé dish and then dust it with sugar.

In a heavy saucepan over a low heat, melt the chocolate with the milk, stirring with a wooden spoon until it is blended and smooth. Remove from the heat and whisk in ⅔ cup of the sugar, the vanilla, salt, and espresso powder. Whisk in the egg yolks, one at a time.

To the bowl of an electric stand mixer, add the egg whites. On medium speed with the whisk attachment, beat the egg whites, adding the remaining ¼ cup sugar and the cream of tartar gradually, until they stand in soft peaks.

Transfer the chocolate base to a large mixing bowl and add about a quarter of the egg whites to lighten it and stir it well. Pour in the rest of the egg whites and gently fold them into the chocolate mixture.

Pour into the prepared soufflé dish, and bake it for 20 to 25 minutes until it is just done but still moist. Serve immediately, dusted with powdered sugar and crème anglaise.

Crème Anglaise

YIELD: *3 cups*

6 egg yolks
½ cup sugar
½ teaspoon salt

1 tablespoon flour
2 cups milk
2 teaspoons vanilla extract

In the bowl of an electric stand mixer fitted with the whisk attachment on medium speed, whisk together the egg yolks, sugar, salt, and flour, until the "ribbon" forms, about 5 minutes.

Prepare a double boiler, pour the egg yolk mixture into the top, add the milk, and cook over medium heat until the mixture has just thickened and coats the back of a spoon, 8 to 10 minutes. If you see the first sign of a simmer, stop immediately.

Strain the sauce into a bowl and stir in the vanilla, and save it to reheat it or serve immediately.

This soufflé is so easy you won't need Mark, Nora, or Mike to help you!

Strawberry Cobbler

IN THE early 1990s, Julia Child came to The Patio by the River for a dinner honoring herself and Robert Mondavi, founders of the American Institute of Wine and Food. We served a traditional Southern barbecue: Brunswick stew, cole slaw, barbecued chicken, potato salad, and strawberry cobbler with vanilla ice cream. Julia told me this dish was her very favorite strawberry dish of all time. It's mine, too. An added plus: there is almost nothing easier to make. Serve it warm with vanilla ice cream.

YIELD: *8 to 10 servings*

2 sticks (16 tablespoons) salted butter, melted

4 cups whole strawberries, stemmed (frozen strawberries certainly are convenient . . .)

2 cups flour

1 tablespoon baking soda

1 teaspoon salt

2 cups sugar

2 cups milk

Preheat the oven to 350°F.

Pour the melted butter into a 13 × 9 × 2-inch baking dish, and add the strawberries.

In a large mixing bowl, whisk together the flour, baking soda, salt, and sugar, and then slowly add the milk, whisking it until it is smooth.

Pour the batter over the fruit and bake for 45 minutes, until it's more than golden brown and set. Serve the cobbler warm with vanilla ice cream.

On the banks of the Chattahoochee: (left to right) Harry Hataway, Julia Child, Jan Shackleford, and Mary Boyle Hataway at The Patio by the River, fall 1992

Dorothy's Coconut Cake

COCONUT ENTHUSIASTS rejoice! You have arrived at Mecca! Although she made it all the time, Dorothy didn't have a written recipe for this one, so circa 1980 my mother made it with her and wrote the whole thing down. I have enhanced it for this book, and now it's Coconut Cake Extreme, just for you.

YIELD: *One 9-inch cake, approximately 16 servings*

CAKE

6 tablespoons cold salted butter, plus
    more for the pans
2½ cups cake flour, plus more for
    the pans
2¼ cups sugar
1½ tablespoons vanilla extract
1 stick (8 tablespoons) salted butter,
    melted
5 egg yolks

3 eggs
1 tablespoon salt
1 tablespoon baking powder
½ cup buttermilk
¾ cup heavy cream

GLAZE

½ cup coconut milk
2 tablespoons powdered sugar

Preheat the oven to 325°F. Butter and flour three 9-inch cake pans, put a parchment round in the bottom of each pan, and butter and flour the rounds.

Beat the cold butter in the bowl of an electric stand mixer fitted with the paddle attachment on medium speed, until it is very light, about 5 minutes. Continue beating while gradually adding the sugar, scraping down the sides of the bowl as necessary.

Add the vanilla and beat for 5 more minutes, scraping down the sides of the bowl again. The mixture will be very coarse and grainy. Turn the mixer to the lowest speed, add the melted butter, egg yolks, and eggs, and then turn off the mixer.

In a large bowl, sift together the flour, salt, and baking powder.

In another bowl, mix the buttermilk and cream together.

With the mixer on the lowest speed, add half of the flour, and then half of the buttermilk mixture. Then add the remaining flour mixture and the remaining buttermilk mixture, scraping down the sides of the bowl as necessary. Do not overmix or the cake will be tough.

Pour the batter evenly into the prepared pans, and tap each pan on a sturdy surface to release the air bubbles if there are any, and bake it for 25 to 30 minutes, until a toothpick or knife comes out clean.

Cool the cakes for 10 minutes, then run the dull edge of a knife around the perimeter of the pans and invert them onto a cold baking sheet or rack. Note: these cakes may be frozen for up to 3 months at this point.

When you are ready to ice the cake, slice each layer horizontally in half so that you have 6 layers.

To make the glaze, whisk together the powdered sugar and coconut milk in a small bowl. Pierce each layer of the cake with a fork in several places and then spoon or brush the glaze over each layer before icing it.

Make sure all the layers are completely cool before you ice them.

COCONUT ICING

1½ cups fresh or dried coconut, shredded

18 ounces cream cheese, at room temperature

18 tablespoons salted butter, at room temperature

3 tablespoons vanilla extract

7½ cups powdered sugar

2¼ teaspoons salt

6 tablespoons coconut milk

5⅓ cups sweetened flaked coconut

Preheat the oven to 350°F.

Spread the fresh or dried coconut on a metal baking sheet and toast for about 5 to 7 minutes, until it is brown. Remove from the oven and reserve.

In the bowl of an electric stand mixer fitted with the paddle attachment on medium speed, combine the cream cheese, butter, and vanilla extract, and beat for about 5 minutes, until it is light and fluffy.

In a large mixing bowl, combine the powdered sugar and salt, and add it to the cream cheese mixture, 1 cup at a time, beating it until it is smooth after each addition. Turn the mixer to the lowest speed, add the coconut milk, and stir in the sweetened flaked coconut. Arrange the cooled layers, one by one, on a cake stand, icing each layer as you assemble, using approximately 1 cup of icing per layer, and then top with the toasted coconut.

Coconut Pudding with Caramel Sauce

MY FRIEND Susan Gutfreund is an excellent hostess. She decorates beautifully, too. And she can cook. In theatrical circles, one might call her a "triple threat"! One Christmas Eve, she served me this incredible pudding, and I asked her about the recipe so I could include it in this book. So delicious and so versatile, as it can be paired with a red fruit coulis, a chocolate sauce, or, my favorite, this caramel sauce. She told me its origin was another friend, Betsy Bloomingdale (see pages 239, 244, and 309), from her own cookbook, and here's what Susan had done to make small changes in it, et cetera . . . I adapted it for this book, have served it again and again, and the combination of the caramel and the coconut is unexpected and extraordinary.

Susan Gutfreund at home in New York, circa 2006

NOTE There is no question that this recipe would be better with fresh coconut, but I am neither diligent nor quite patient enough. I use both dried unsweetened coconut, softened in water, and sweetened coconut for the pudding and for garnish.

YIELD: *About 6 cups, or 8 servings*

1 cup sweetened coconut
2 cups half-and-half
1½ cups sugar
½ teaspoon salt
2 tablespoons unflavored gelatin
1 cup cold water
1 teaspoon almond extract

2½ cups grated coconut (unsweetened, dried, softened in warm water, and measured after draining)
3 cups heavy cream
3 tablespoons powdered sugar
Caramel Sauce (recipe follows)

Preheat the oven to 350°F.

Spread ½ cup of the sweetened coconut on a metal baking sheet and toast it for about 5 minutes, until it is brown. Remove from the oven and reserve.

In a heavy saucepan over medium heat, bring the half-and-half to a boil. Whisk in the sugar and salt, and then transfer it to a large mixing bowl to let it cool slightly.

In a small mixing bowl, dissolve the gelatin in cold water. Whisk it into the half-and-half, and when the mixture is smooth add the almond extract and the unsweetened coconut.

Whip the cream and the powdered sugar together until stiff peaks form.

Add about a quarter of the whipped cream to the coconut mixture to lighten it, and then fold in the remaining whipped cream. Pour the mixture into a mold or a serving bowl, cover it, and refrigerate it overnight until it's firm. Before serving, top it with the toasted coconut, and serve it with warm caramel sauce.

Caramel Sauce

YIELD: *1½ cups*

2 tablespoons salted butter
1 pound light brown sugar
2 egg yolks
1 cup heavy cream

1 teaspoon salt
1 tablespoon plus 1 teaspoon vanilla
  extract

In a heavy saucepan or double boiler over low heat, melt the butter, brown sugar, egg yolks, heavy cream, and salt until the sugar has dissolved. Be careful not to burn the sugar.

Remove it from the heat, stir in the vanilla, and serve the sauce warm.

FOLLOWING SPREAD *Here's an idea on how to serve the Caramel Sauce: make a small indentation on the top of the unmolded pudding, fill it with sauce, and let it drizzle down the sides, or pass the sauce separately.*

Hummingbird Cake
with Cream Cheese Icing

IS THIS a spice cake? An Italian wedding cake? A fruit cake? Nope. It's a nineteenth-century Southern delicacy, laden with pecans, bananas, and pineapples, and utterly addictive in every way. I found this recipe in a series of yellowed index cards in a box from circa 1920 with what I believe to be my great-grandmother's handwriting on it, hauled it out, and made it. I couldn't believe how good it was. I tweaked the icing a bit and, voilà! Hummingbird cake! Don't you just love the name?

YIELD: *One 9-inch cake, about 16 servings*

3 cups chopped pecans, mixed with
 ¼ teaspoon salt
3¼ teaspoons salt, divided
Butter for the pans
6 cups all-purpose flour, plus
 more for the pans
2 teaspoons baking soda
4 cups sugar
2 teaspoons ground cinnamon
6 large eggs, beaten
4 sticks (32 tablespoons) salted
 butter, melted

1 tablespoon plus 1 teaspoon
 vanilla extract
2 (8-ounce) cans crushed pineapple,
 undrained
4 cups chopped bananas
Cream Cheese Icing (recipe follows)
1 cup chopped pecans, toasted
 at 350° for approximately
 5 minutes, with ¼ teaspoon salt,
 for garnish

Preheat the oven to 350°F.

Spread 1 cup of the chopped pecans on a metal baking sheet and then sprinkle them with ¼ teaspoon of the salt. Roast the pecans for approximately 5 minutes, until they are browner but not burned. Remove them from the oven and reserve.

Butter and flour three 9-inch cake pans, put a parchment round in the bottom of each pan, and butter and flour the rounds.

Whisk together the flour, baking soda, the remaining 3 teaspoons salt, sugar, and cinnamon in a large mixing bowl. Add the beaten eggs and melted butter and stir until the dry ingredients are just moistened. Do not beat the batter or the cake will be tough.

(continued on next page)

(continued from previous page)

Stir in the vanilla, pineapple, bananas, and the remaining 2 cups pecans.

Pour the batter equally into the pans and bake for 25 to 30 minutes, until a knife or toothpick comes out clean.

Cool the cakes on a rack for 10 minutes, then run a knife around the edges of the pans and invert them onto a cold baking sheet to remove the cakes from the pans. When they have cooled completely, assemble the cakes neatly on a cake stand and ice each layer with the cream cheese icing. Each layer should have approximately one cup of icing.

Add the roasted pecans to the top of the iced cake, and serve.

Cream Cheese Icing

18 ounces cream cheese, at room temperature

18 tablespoons salted butter, at room temperature

3 tablespoons vanilla extract

7½ cups powdered sugar

2¼ teaspoons salt

Beat the cream cheese, butter, and vanilla in the bowl of an electric stand mixer fitted with the paddle attachment on medium speed for about 5 minutes, until it is light and fluffy.

In a large mixing bowl, combine the powdered sugar and salt, then add it to the cream cheese mixture, 1 cup at a time, beating after each addition until it is smooth.

Luscious Lemon-Ginger Squares

TELENA STRIPLING SAXTON is a *force majeure*. Good-humored, loving, saucy, and with a profound sense of the dramatic, Telena is one of Atlanta's great characters. In the food world, we would say that she has "the touch." When I asked her how she learned to cook she told me, "We were thirteen growing up. If you didn't cook, you didn't eat!" Her "growing up" was in a picturesque middle Georgia town called Washington-Wilkes, known for its genteel entertaining and delicious food. Any time my parents entertained more than ten or twelve people, which they did thirty or forty times a year, Telena came to oversee the kitchen. She was a personal chef before there really was such a thing, and she was the not-so-secret secret of many successful parties of Atlanta's carriage trade. Once, when my mother's ovens went on the fritz during a seated lunch for forty people, I saw Telena finish six or eight large cheese soufflés on top of the stove in a bain-marie, and no one, not even the hostess, was any the wiser.

Telena's menus for big buffet parties often ended with what she referred to as the "sweet tray." That tray consisted of pecan tarts, sugar timbales, brownies, and these luscious lemon squares. I have always loved Telena and was thrilled to help in the kitchen, starting at about age four. She sometimes let me arrange the assorted desserts on silver platters before she gave them a generous sprinkling of powdered sugar to pretty them up. To quote her, she "stood up over" me one day, and the result was horrifying. She delivered an admonition I will never forget, and one I use to this day. "Boy," she said sternly, "you ought' know better than this. Don't bring me no skimpy platters!"

YIELD: *2 to 3 dozen squares, depending on the size you cut them*

CRUST
2 sticks (16 tablespoons) salted butter, cold, plus more for the baking pan

½ cup powdered sugar
1¾ cups all-purpose flour
2 tablespoons minced fresh ginger
¼ teaspoon salt

Preheat the oven to 350°F. Butter a 9 × 13-inch metal baking pan.

In the bowl of an electric stand mixer fitted with the paddle attachment,

(continued on next page)

(continued from previous page)

on medium speed, cream the butter and sugar together until they are light, approximately 5 minutes. Turn the mixture to the lowest speed and stir in the flour, ginger, and salt until you have coarse crumbs.

Pour the crumbs into the buttered baking pan and press them down with your fingers to fully cover the pan. Bake the crust for 25 minutes, until it is golden brown and cooked through. Let cool.

LEMON TOPPING

6 large eggs
2½ cups plus 2 tablespoons sugar
7 tablespoons fresh lemon juice
¼ teaspoon salt
1 teaspoon baking powder
¼ cup plus ½ teaspoon all-purpose
   flour

In a large mixing bowl, whisk together the eggs and sugar. Add the lemon juice, salt, and baking powder, and then whisk in the flour until it is thoroughly combined.

Pour the mixture over the pre-baked, cooled crust, and bake it for 25 to 30 minutes, until it is just set.

Again, bake these in a 9 × 13-inch metal baking pan and cut them to whatever shape you want before you serve them. Note: these freeze beautifully and are much easier to cut when they are frozen.

Betsy's Peach Ice Cream

LEAVE IT to a Californian to teach this Georgia peach about peach ice cream. I refer here again to Betsy Bloomingdale, a self-proclaimed foodie and cookbook author, and one of the best hostesses in America. I had this homemade ice cream in the height of summer peach season several years ago and had to have the recipe. The secret ingredient here is almond extract, which provides a lovely undertone, supporting the main flavors beautifully without ever stealing the spotlight.

YIELD: *2 quarts, about 8 servings*

6 medium super-ripe peaches,
   and I mean super-ripe!
1½ cups sugar
1½ tablespoons lemon juice

3 cups heavy cream
¾ teaspoon salt
1 tablespoon vanilla extract
1 teaspoon almond extract

Peel the peaches and remove their pits.

In a food processor fitted with the metal blade, puree the peaches and transfer them to a mixing bowl. Add the sugar and lemon juice, and stir the mixture well to combine. Cover and refrigerate for 2 hours.

In a medium-sized mixing bowl, whisk together the cream, salt, vanilla, and almond extract, and stir in the peach mixture.

Transfer the ice cream base to the container of an ice cream freezer, and freeze it according to the manufacturer's directions.

Priceless Pecan Bars

IF PECAN bars had a gold standard, this would be it. I have never, ever had any better. So many pecan pie–like things are made with corn syrup—a practice I cannot ever see as acceptable in my kitchen. I have replaced that product with sugar, eggs, and butter, and if they aren't the best you've ever had, please send me your recipe, and we'll test them together, because I just don't believe you!

YIELD: *One 9 × 13 baking pan, or one quarter sheet pan*

CRUST

2 sticks (16 tablespoons) salted butter, cold, plus more for the baking pan

1½ cups dark brown sugar, firmly packed

2 cups flour

½ teaspoon salt

PECAN TOPPING

4 large eggs

1½ cups dark brown sugar, firmly packed

½ teaspoon salt

1 tablespoon plus 1 teaspoon vanilla extract

1½ cups chopped pecans

Preheat the oven to 350°F. Butter a 9 × 13-inch metal baking pan.

To make the crust, in the bowl of an electric stand mixer fitted with the paddle attachment on medium speed, cream the butter and sugar together until they are light, about 5 minutes.

Turn the mixer to low and add the flour and salt, mixing them until you have coarse crumbs.

Pour the crumbs into the prepared baking pan and press them down with your fingers to cover the pan evenly.

Bake the crust for 20 minutes, until it is just brown, remove it from the oven, and let it cool completely.

To make the topping, in the bowl of an electric stand mixer fitted with the whisk attachment on low speed beat the eggs and sugar together until they are smooth, approximately 3 to 5 minutes.

Turn the mixer to the lowest speed, and add the salt, vanilla, and chopped pecans. Turn the mixer off.

Pour the pecan topping over the cooled crust and bake it for 25 to 30 minutes, until it is just set.

Pecan Shortbread Cookies

THIS RECIPE is inspired by Master Baker Eli Zabar's shortbread recipe, and there seems to be a version of it in every culture. In Mexico, it's called a wedding cookie; in France (literally translated), a sand tart; in Scotland, shortbread. I add pecans and call it seriously delicious. More often than not, I serve these passed with coffee after dinner.

YIELD: *About 4 dozen small cookies*

3 sticks (24 tablespoons) salted
    butter, cold
1 cup sugar
2 teaspoons vanilla extract

3½ cups flour
⅛ teaspoon salt
1 cup chopped pecans
Powdered sugar

Preheat the oven to 350°F. Line a 9 × 13-inch metal baking sheet with parchment paper.

In the bowl of an electric stand mixer fitted with the paddle attachment on medium speed, cream the butter and sugar together for approximately 3 to 5 minutes, and then add the vanilla.

In a medium mixing bowl, whisk the flour and salt together. Turn the mixer to the lowest speed and stir in the flour mixture. Then add the chopped pecans and turn the mixer off.

Put the dough in the refrigerator and let it cool for 30 minutes. Using whatever size scoop you want, scoop the dough onto the prepared baking sheet and bake for 15 to 20 minutes.

Let the cookies cool completely, dredge them generously in powdered sugar, and serve.

Pecan Shortbread Cookies go with everything.

Pineapple Upside-Down Cake
with Hot Rum Sauce

THERE WAS an online story done about my entertaining and food several months ago for an Italian magazine, and of all the desserts I offered them, they chose this one. They thought it sounded really American. We did literally dozens of iterations of it, and the entire crew couldn't wait for one after the next, topped with Hot Rum Sauce, fresh from the oven. It really couldn't be easier, and requires virtually no skill of any kind. Take credit for it as if it did.

YIELD: *One 9-inch cake*

PINEAPPLE TOPPING
½ ripe medium pineapple, peeled, cored, and eyes removed
1 stick (8 tablespoons) salted butter
¼ teaspoon salt
1 cup dark brown sugar, firmly packed
1 tablespoon dark rum

CAKE
1 cup cake flour
1 cup all-purpose flour
1½ cups sugar
1¼ teaspoons baking soda
1 teaspoon baking powder
¾ teaspoon salt
1 cup buttermilk
2 eggs
2 teaspoons vanilla extract
2 tablespoons dark rum
1 stick (8 tablespoons) salted butter, melted
Hot Rum Sauce (recipe follows)

Preheat the oven to 375°F.

To make the topping, cut the pineapple into ½-inch rounds and then cut the rounds into ¾-inch pieces.

Combine the butter, salt, sugar, and rum in a heavy 9-inch cake pan or a cast-iron skillet over medium heat and cook until it bubbles, 4 to 5 minutes. Remove from the heat and let cool for no more than 2 minutes.

(continued on next page)

OPPOSITE *Drizzling the Hot Rum Sauce over the Pineapple Upside-Down Cake*

(continued from previous page)

Arrange the pineapple slices in the bottom of the cake pan evenly and in an attractive geometric pattern.

To make the cake, in a large mixing bowl, whisk together the cake flour, all-purpose flour, sugar, baking soda, baking powder, and salt. Then add the buttermilk, eggs, vanilla, dark rum, and melted butter, and whisk them together until a batter just forms, but be careful not to blend too well. This undermixing will explain the cake's exquisite dense but tender texture.

Pour the batter over the pineapple and caramel mixture, place the cake pan on a baking sheet, as some of the batter will inevitably spill over during baking, and bake for 40 to 45 minutes.

Remove the cake from the oven and let it cool for 4 minutes exactly, and run the blunt edge of a knife around the sides of the pan to loosen the cake.

Invert the hot cake onto a serving platter and let cool for at least 20 minutes before serving it warm with the hot rum sauce.

Hot Rum Sauce

YIELD: *2 cups*

2 cups heavy cream
1½ cups sugar
1 tablespoon vanilla extract

1 teaspoon salt
3 tablespoons dark rum

In a medium heavy saucepan over medium heat, bring all the ingredients to a boil, whisking occasionally to combine, and then turn off the heat. Strain the sauce through a fine sieve. Serve it warm or at room temperature.

OPPOSITE, TOP LEFT *Melt the butter and sugar together over medium heat.* OPPOSITE, TOP RIGHT *When the butter and sugar begin to bubble, immediately remove them from the heat. Then add the salt and the rum.* OPPOSITE, BOTTOM *Arrange the cut pineapple in a geometric pattern as this upside-down bottom will become the top of your cake.*

Perfect Poached Pears in Red Wine

THESE ARE utterly elegant, beautiful, and delicious. I often serve them as a light dessert for lunch. They are equally good warm or cold, but I truly love them warm, on a cold winter's day, with whipped cream and lots of that incredibly sumptuous, deep-ruby-colored sauce spooned all over the top.

YIELD: *8 servings*

1¾ cups sugar
1 bottle red wine
1 cinnamon stick

¼ teaspoon salt
2 pounds firm pears
1 tablespoon lemon juice

Simmer the sugar, wine, cinnamon stick, and salt together in a large, heavy stockpot over medium heat for about 5 minutes, until it has had time to steep. Do not boil this mixture.

Peel the pears, cut them in half lengthwise, and core them. Add the pears to the liquid in one layer, and gently poach them for 10 to 12 minutes, spooning the wine over them from the beginning so that they will color evenly.

When they are fork-tender all the way through (I recommend that you check them after 8 minutes or so), remove them from the poaching liquid with a slotted spoon. Place them on a baking sheet, and let them cool while you finish the sauce. If you are serving them later, cover and refrigerate until they are cool.

Turn the heat up to high and boil the poaching liquid until it reaches a syrupy consistency, about 20 to 25 minutes. Remove from the heat and stir in the lemon juice.

Spoon the sauce over the pears and serve.

Sweet Potato Pie

THIS IS so full-flavored and so easy. I will venture to say that even if you don't love sweet potatoes, which, if I were to be honest, I would tell you that I don't, you will love this pie. It is simply that good.

YIELD: *One 9-inch pie*

1½ pounds sweet potatoes
1 cup heavy cream
½ cup brown sugar
½ cup good maple syrup
½ cup sugar
5 tablespoons salted butter, melted
3 eggs, beaten
¼ cup bourbon

½ teaspoon ground cinnamon
¾ teaspoon salt
½ teaspoon ground nutmeg
⅛ teaspoon ground cloves
⅛ teaspoon ground black pepper
½ teaspoon ground ginger
½ Pâte Brisée recipe (page 268)

Preheat the oven to 425°F.

Place the sweet potatoes on a baking sheet, pierce them with a fork all over, and roast for 1 hour. Remove them from the oven, peel them, and put them in a large mixing bowl. Mash with a potato masher until they are smooth.

Turn the oven down to 325°F.

Add all of the other ingredients to the mashed sweet potatoes and stir well to combine. Pour into the prebaked pâte brisée shell, and bake for 50 minutes.

Remove from the oven and serve it warm or cold.

White Chocolate Mint Mousse

ONE LOOK, and you'll know that green crème de menthe is an ingredient. It's got that amazing pale green color—and honestly, I find this dessert addictive. I have so much fun serving this as a layer on top of my traditional Chocolate Mousse (page 294), then covered with shaved or chopped white and dark chocolate. It's almost too pretty to eat.

YIELD: *2 quarts, or 6 to 8 servings*

MASTER LIST OF INGREDIENTS

8 egg yolks
1½ cups plus 4 tablespoons sugar, divided
¾ cup crème de menthe, divided
¼ teaspoon salt, divided
12 ounces white chocolate

2 tablespoons vanilla extract
2½ cups heavy cream, divided
2 sticks (16 tablespoons) salted butter, cold, cut into quarters
2 tablespoons unflavored gelatin
2 tablespoons water

---

8 egg yolks
1½ cups sugar

½ cup crème de menthe (green!)
⅛ teaspoon salt

In the bowl of a large electric stand mixer fitted with the whisk attachment, on medium speed beat all these ingredients together until the "ribbon" forms, approximately 5 minutes.

Prepare a double boiler and pour the mixture in. Cook until it is ever so slightly thickened and too hot to touch. Do not overcook this mixture, or you will have green scrambled eggs.

12 ounces white chocolate
2 tablespoons vanilla extract

½ cup heavy cream

In a medium heavy saucepan over low heat, combine all the above ingredients and melt them slowly, stirring constantly. Let it cool for about 3 minutes.

In an electric stand mixer fitted with the whisk attachment on medium

(continued on next page)

OPPOSITE *White Chocolate Mint Mousse over a layer of Chocolate Mousse*

(continued from previous page)

speed, beat the white chocolate mixture and egg mixture together for approximately 4 to 5 minutes, until fully combined. Add

> 2 sticks (16 tablespoons) salted
> butter, cold, cut into quarters

and beat the mixture until the butter is fully incorporated. Transfer the mousse base into a large mixing bowl and wash the bowl of your electric mixer.

Back to the electric mixer: with the whisk attachment fitted, beat

> 2 cups heavy cream   ⅛ teaspoon salt
> 4 tablespoons sugar

until stiff peaks form, and fold the whipped cream into the mousse base. In a small mixing bowl, dissolve

> 2 tablespoons unflavored gelatin in
> ¼ cup green crème de menthe
> and 2 tablespoons water

and stir the dissolved gelatin into the mixture, mixing it well. Pour the mousse into a serving bowl, cover, and refrigerate it overnight.

Shave or finely chop some white and dark chocolate to use as garnish for these mousses.

Bourbon Whipped Cream

THIS RECIPE is elegant, flavorful, easy, and memorable—in other words, the very best way to end a lunch or dinner. It's perfect on just about anything, so let your imagination run wild, but I especially like it on top of Molten Chocolate Cake (page 292), Peggy's Apricot Mousse (page 279), or as a decadently rich complement to plain fresh berries.

YIELD: *1½ cups, or 6 to 8 servings*

1 cup heavy cream
¼ cup sugar
2 tablespoons good-quality bourbon
    (I like Maker's Mark or Wild
    Turkey)

In the bowl of an electric stand mixer fitted with the whisk attachment, combine all the ingredients. Whip on medium speed until the desired texture is achieved—I like soft peaks for this recipe.

Serve over everything!

Connie's Chocolate Sauce

I WAS introduced to Connie Wald by friends when I first went to Los Angeles. For the past six or seven decades her lunches and dinners have included a who's who of Hollywood. At Connie's I have shared evenings with the varied likes of Olivia de Havilland, Gore Vidal, Natasha Richardson and Liam Neeson, Julian Sands, Samuel Goldwyn, Roddy McDowall, and on and on and on, if you see what I mean. Connie is generous, loyal, caring, and beloved. We often discuss food and recipes, and I am very lucky that she has shared some of her guests' and my favorites with me for this book. Connie credits Mildred Knopf with this formula for the easiest and most delicious chocolate sauce, so scrumptious that Gloria Stewart (Mrs. Jimmy) "wanted to rub it in her hair!"

LEFT TO RIGHT *Rocky (Mrs. Gary) Cooper, Maureen O'Hara, Jimmy Stewart, Rosalind Russell, Gloria Stewart, Jerry Wald, Connie Wald, and Maria Cooper at the premiere of* Mr. Hobbs Takes a Vacation, *June 1962*

4 ounces unsweetened chocolate

1 tablespoon salted butter

1 cup sugar

¼ teaspoon salt

½ cup half-and-half

1 tablespoon vanilla extract

In a double boiler over medium-low heat, melt the chocolate and butter together.

In a mixing bowl, whisk together the sugar, salt, and half-and-half, then add it to the chocolate mixture, and cook until the sugar has fully dissolved.

Stir in the vanilla extract and serve the sauce over vanilla ice cream (or just about anything else).

Sauce Sabayon

IN EUROPE, there's a similar sauce in every country. In Italy, it's zabaglione, in France, it's Sauce Sabayon. This sauce is easy, and the ultimate, elegant answer to dress up fresh berries in summer or as a filling for a cream cake when the seasons call for heavier layers of clothing.

YIELD: *About 2 cups, or 8 to 12 servings*

8 egg yolks

1 teaspoon salt

1 cup sugar

Juice of ½ lemon (about
    1½ tablespoons)

1 cup sherry

2 teaspoons brandy

1 cup heavy cream, whipped

In the bowl of an electric stand mixer fitted with the whisk attachment on medium speed, beat the egg yolks, salt, sugar, and lemon juice together until they are light, about 5 minutes.

Prepare a double boiler over medium heat and pour the mixture into the top. Add the sherry and brandy and stir the sauce constantly until it's thick, 10 to 12 minutes.

Cool the mixture, transfer it to a mixing bowl, and fold in the whipped cream.

Serve over anything!

12

Entertaining and Menus

Planning menus should always be influenced by the season, celebrating the freshest ingredients during their peak times. For these menus I've chosen recipes that best reflect the glories of each and every season, ones that I've used for many successful parties. When planning a menu, it's important to balance flavors and choose dishes that complement one another rather than fight for attention—and please, *never ever* repeat main ingredients from one course to the next.

Remember that when you entertain, as important as the food, service, and atmosphere is, parties are about people. To be a successful host or hostess is to be a watchmaker: make it, wind it up, and watch it go. Plan your parties to the limit, sweat the small stuff, and then get everything done ahead of time, so you can relax and enjoy your guests. A stressed host won't accomplish anything except making his guests really uncomfortable, and then, unfortunately, no one has a good time!

Spring

I used this spring menu for a seated dinner for fourteen that I hosted last year. Please note that I served the main course as a first course, and then followed it with a salad and cheese course as if we were in France:

- Seven-Hour Lamb
- Gratin Dauphinois
- A simple green salad with Dijon Mustard Vinaigrette and cheese
- Perfect Poached Pears in Red Wine

The heartiness of this next menu is cut by the freshness of the asparagus, and I find the spice-cake-like dessert a welcome contrapunto to the main flavors of the menu.

- Shrimp Bisque
- Osso Buco
- Caroline's Soubise
- Perfect Asparagus
- Hummingbird Cake with Cream Cheese Icing

Or one of my absolute favorite dinners:

- Spinach Soufflé
- Pecan-Crusted Salmon with Sauce Gribiche
- My Hash Brown Cake
- Pineapple Upside-Down Cake with Hot Rum Sauce

If there were a perfect lunch menu, this one may very well be it:

- Four-Cheese Soufflé
- Dover Sole Florentine
- Oven-Roasted Tomatoes
- Chocolate Mousse

Summer

During the summer, I usually give larger parties, as the tables can easily spill outside because of the lovely California weather. I used this menu for a birthday dinner for thirty people last summer; the only substitution made here is my Strawberry Cobbler instead of the delicious birthday cake I actually served.

- Cold Cucumber Soup
- Sautéed Chilean Sea Bass with Beurre Blanc
- Silver Queen Corn Pudding
- Strawberry Cobbler with vanilla ice cream

This reminds me of a late August evening, just as the days start to shorten, but when it's still nice and hot at noon and then cool at night:

- Cold Avocado Soup
- Parmesan-Crusted Chicken with Lemon Butter
- Red Pepper Flan
- Spinach salad
- Fresh berries with Sauce Sabayon

Or this easy, light, summer picnic, served cold:

- Swordfish Kebobs with Tomatoes, Peppers, and Onions with 1, 2, 3 Vinaigrette
- Rice Salad
- Magnificent Broccoli Puree
- Luscious Lemon-Ginger Squares

A summer dinner with dressed-up guests. In other words, a fancy dinner with not-so-fancy food:

- My Smoked Salmon Tartare on Cucumber Rounds
- Dorothy's Fried Chicken
- Broccoli Slaw
- Dorothy's Squash Casserole
- Best-Ever Brownies

Fall

This fall dinner menu is great for six or sixty, an easy do-ahead series of dishes, actually much better when prepared the day before:

- Butternut Squash Soup
- Robert's Favorite Turkey Hash
- A simple green salad with Dijon Mustard Vinaigrette
- New Orleans Bread Pudding with Vanilla Bourbon Sauce

This is an extraordinary lunch menu:

- Gratin of Spinach Fettuccine with Ham and Onions
- Quail Salad with Lentil Vinaigrette and Goat Cheese Crostini
- Sweet Potato Pie

Here's another one for fall, which was done for a friend's birthday. It was a buffet for thirty-six and was a huge hit:

- Roulade of Pheasant Breast Stuffed with Spinach and Mushroom Duxelles
- Pumpkin Pecan Flan with Roquefort
- Bibb lettuce and chive salad with Red Wine Vinaigrette
- Apple and Pear Crumble with Maple Cinnamon Ice Cream

I absolutely love the two purees together, and find the chasseur sauce an excellent accompaniment to both:

- Oyster Stew
- Chicken Chasseur
- Carrot Puree with Ginger
- Magnificent Broccoli Puree
- Chocolate Mousse

OPPOSITE, ABOVE RIGHT *Tony Rivero and Alberto Gonzales, who have helped me at every party I've ever given in Los Angeles*

Winter

For a small and elegant winter dinner these delicious choices will keep your guests warm. There's nothing like comfort food to feed the soul, and I've served this menu time and again during the colder months.

- Lobster Bisque
- Perfect Roast Tenderloin of Beef with Béarnaise Sauce
- Caroline's Soubise, Red Pepper Flan, steamed broccoli
- Chocolate Soufflé with Crème Anglaise

Or this marvelous menu, ideal for lunch or dinner. One note: if you serve this at night, add a scoop of vanilla ice cream to the pecan bars. It's probably too heavy for the daytime . . .

- Smoked Salmon Crêpes with Beurre Blanc
- Chicken Country Captain
- Priceless Pecan Bars

And this one, a January spectacular, just deep enough in the month so that people are very hungry from all their post-Christmas dieting and ready for a hearty dinner.

- Mushroom Soup
- Erlinda's Exquisite Short Ribs
- Dorothy's Baked Cheddar Grits
- Perfect Asparagus
- Coconut Pudding with Caramel Sauce

An evening menu with so many great flavors, all of them much better when done ahead:

- "She" Crab Soup
- Billionaire's Meatloaf
- Mashed Potatoes with Maytag Blue
- A simple green salad with 1, 2, 3 Vinaigrette
- Salted Caramel Cake

Index

Page numbers in *italics* refer to illustrations.

A NOTE ABOUT THE AUTHOR

Alex Hitz lives in Los Angeles and
New York. This is his first book.

A NOTE ON THE TYPE

The text of this book was set in Sabon,
a typeface designed by Jan Tschichold
(1902–1974).

Composed by
North Market Street Graphics,
Lancaster, Pennsylvania

Printed and bound by Toppan,
China

Designed by Maggie Hinders